UNCONDITIONAL LOVE

FOR HUMANITY

The New Earth

By Jerry Alatalo

ISBN-13:978-1481092432

These writings are dedicated to humanity. Thank you to all men, women and children on this beautiful planet. Thank you for your efforts on behalf of your brothers and sisters in the family of man. Thank you for creating The New Earth.

CONTENTS.

I. REASONS.

II. BEING HUMAN.

"Let a man in a garret but burn with enough intensity and he will set fire to the whole world... I know of but one freedom and that is the freedom of the mind. Truth, for any man, is that which makes him a man." –Antoine de Saint-Exupery

I. Reasons.

A. Let a man in a garret but burn...

Thank you for reading these words.

The reason we are writing these words is that now is the time to end human suffering.

My name is Jerry Alatalo and I live on Lake Superior in the Upper Peninsula of Michigan, United States of America. We hope that our writings help everyone, everywhere on Earth. We pray that all will find unconditional Love and join in the effort to create a Heaven on Earth.

We would like to say at the outset here that the writer is human just as we all are. The ideas and thoughts used by the writer are interpretive and he admits that interpreting spiritual information is subject to error. One runs into ideas and concepts that could be termed recondite. The definition of recondite is dealing with very profound, difficult, or abstruse subject matter. The definition of interpret is to explain the meaning of. The writer is not a guru, saint, enlightened being, yogi or spiritual adept but a simple human being trying to make some sense of our common, human experiencing of life.

Perhaps your interpretations will vary with the writer's. This is ok. We all have our paths to travel and they are somewhat different journeys for all of us. We want you to know that our ideas and thoughts will be expressed as honestly as possible. As we are delving into the concept of God or what some call the Great Mystery there is an obvious inability to truly describe such an overwhelmingly tremendous subject.

An exploration into the truth of our existence is a bold action. We would applaud all human beings who at this time are making the same efforts to learn their truths in order to create a better world. This is a process that every soul will go through and we are humbled to contribute in any way that helps others in their spiritual search. We are excited that humanity is now willing to rise to the truth of unconditional Love. There is the sense that great changes are occurring and that things are only going to get better for humanity as we all move ahead.

These writings are a direct communication from the writer to his brothers and sisters of what is occurring in his days on the spiritual level. As we are all on the same journey through life perhaps there will be some agreement on what is found to be the closest observation of literal, spiritual truth. The vision of humanity in agreement on absolute truth drives this effort, with a desire to help create the best world possible for this and future generations.

One could read a thousand more books on spiritual matters before beginning to share ideas and thoughts with others. But there is no time like the present when it comes to the creation of a new and better world for humanity, our Mother Earth and all things.

The one and only purpose of this work is to help our fellow men, women and children.

Perhaps one reader will walk away from this work thankful that they were not the only one who has thought in a certain way. If this is the one and only good result that comes from this effort then the writer can say that the effort has not been in vain.

We hope that after reading this work you will be burning with enough intensity that you will set fire to the entire world. Antoine de Saint-Exupery was a French writer who lived from 1900-1944. He passed on to spirit in an airplane crash during the Second World War.

Forty four years old was the writer de Saint-Exupery when he passed on to the world of spirit. We are thankful to have lived long enough to have been able to share ideas with others. We began writing in 2011 and have been humbled by the process of being as honest as possible with not only you the reader but with oneself.

Put simply we are trying to spread the good news that unconditional Love is the answer to all of the problems that humanity faces on this Earth. The title of this work is Unconditional Love for Humanity. There are two ways to interpret the title; as a noun or as a verb. The first way is that which sees the Creator building into every human being the substance unconditional Love. 'God created unconditional Love for humanity.'

The second way is that which has human beings feeling the unconditional Love that the Creator has given and showing it to all of humanity. 'Humans feel unconditional Love for humanity and all living things.'

A few paragraphs about writing styles. Writing has turned out to be an enjoyable experience. Free thought is a characteristic of individuals whose opinions are formed on the basis of an understanding and rejection of tradition, authority or established belief. Not being the type of writer that comes up with a meticulous plan for a work, we are freethinking in our writing style.

In matters concerning spirituality we hold that our answers are most successfully found inside of us. This perspective breaks with tradition in that many religious organizations assert that these answers are to be found outside, or externally.

Perhaps you are familiar with the concept of improvisation. Most popularly practiced by actors, improvisation calls for no script but the actors invent the dialogue and situations as they go along. We would consider our writing style to be improvisational.

In the world of the musicians they improvise with their instruments or voices and 'riff'. Jimi Hendrix was probably the best known for his improvisational skill on the guitar. Improvisation in the world of music is practiced by those who play instruments as well as by vocalists. Probably the most recognized form of musical improvisation is jazz. It seems that the musician who is excellent at improvising is one who has attained a high degree of expertise with their instrument or voice.

Those who could be considered improvisational in the world of painting would be abstract artists Pablo Picasso, Wassily Kandinsky, Jackson Pollock and others. Artists who improvise choose it because it allows them the freedom to spontaneously create. Many artists feel the need to experiment and see where the spontaneous creating takes them and their audience. These are the men and women artists who have come to a point where the rigid, structured styles expected from them have become too constraining.

One can see spontaneous creators in all kinds of human endeavors. In the arena of sports the spontaneous creators are those athletes who provide the most excitement for the spectators. In football Hall of Fame Detroit Lions running back Barry Sanders comes to mind. Gifted with physical strength, speed and quickness, Sanders was the quintessential jazz runner. Barry Sanders was exciting to watch because he improvised and riffed when he received the football. In the sport of basketball one thinks of little man 5'10" Nate Archibald who one season led the National Basketball Association in both scoring and assists. Archibald used his physical abilities to improvise and riff on the hardwoods, giving the spectators a very exciting experience.

We come full circle here to de Saint-Exupery and his assertion that there is but one freedom, the freedom of the mind. All of the artists and athletes mentioned understand and appreciate the freedom of the mind to create without constraints of any kind. One could say that life is somewhat like a continuous improvisation. All throughout history humanity has been improvising in the sense that freedom of the mind has been responsible for everything that has been created.

So as this writer begins this work he is thoughtful of all those artists who created the wonderful works that audiences appreciated and still appreciate. We wish to produce a work that will be seen one hundred years from now and be appreciated. Not for any type of ego gratification but because if the work is experienced one hundred years from now and is appreciated, then he will have been of some help to humanity.

Ideally the writer will be considered one hundred years from now as part of the large group of people back in 2012 that were joined in the subsequent creation by humanity of The New Earth. We would be remembered for working with many others to build a world where unconditional Love became mankind's basis for a new paradigm, a new way of living. This will be seen by some to be a type of grandiose, wishful thinking. So be it.

We have come to the conclusion that unconditional Love is the answer for humanity's problems.

When one considers all that is happening on this Earth and tries to imagine the possible solutions, and then considers the solution of unconditional Love, there is no longer any doubt. There is no doubt that if unconditional Love were to be grasped by every human being on Earth that humanity's problems would disappear like dew from the grass touched by the rising sun. One wonders how it can be that unconditional Love is not on the minds of everyone. Why has it taken so very long for this answer to be known by all?

How is it that throughout history there has not come a point where everyone on Earth agreed that Love must be the basis for all decision making? The reason that we are doing this work is to contribute in such a way that this point of agreement will be expedited and reached during these times. We will search with all of our strength for the right words and ideas, so that this human condition is successfully brought into reality.

One could say that all of the right words and ideas have been given to humanity through history. Billions of words have been written. Billions of ideas have been shared. Men and women have reached spiritual levels of an extraordinary kind. These men and women have shared their experiences on the mental, physical and spiritual planes in writings for others to consider all along the way. We submit that it is now time to implement the highest wisdom ever revealed through history, everywhere on Earth.

It is time for The New Earth based on unconditional Love and forgiveness.

Many believe that the creation of The New Earth is well underway. We would subscribe to that belief. It would seem that the evolution of humanity has reached that point where there is now an accelerating rise of spiritual awareness and wisdom. Human beings by the millions are every day, week, month and year coming to feel that there is something good coming for the world.

This hope and optimism are signs that the literal creation of a better world is a constantly occurring event. This is an evolution in its naturally occurring state. We are talking specifically here about spiritual evolution. It would seem that the conditions on Earth are improving very rapidly at this time. These improvements are a part of the inevitable march through time by humanity to a new and better world.

Just as we are all born and move through the processes of living, a corresponding process applies to the whole of the human race. We all experience evolution as we grow and attain more knowledge and wisdom. The collective of individual humans, humanity, experiences the same evolutionary process. We may compare the beginnings of mankind to an individual's birth.

Just as individual human beings grow and evolve mankind has also grown and evolved. We are trying to describe how human and collective evolutions coincide.

Just as an individual evolves to that point where there is an awareness of the absolute power of unconditional Love, so also with mankind. With the tremendous increase of individual attainment of awareness of unconditional Love the entire human race collectively is coming to the exact same awareness.

One can use the analogy of any organization that begins with unfamiliarity amongst the group and through time comes to success through good, honest communication. Let us use the example of a high school football team. The team begins with their summer drills and practices. As the teammates, coaches and others communicate and get to know each other the result is an improvement seen every week on the field.

Finally there comes a point where the team plays football at its highest capacity and potential. Lessons are learned about cooperation and what it takes to be successful on the field. This knowledge is added to the knowledge gained by all of those other athletes and coaches ever involved in the game. One would observe that the most important thing for an athlete to learn is to give maximum effort during their performance.

This analogy of sports is seen when one sees the knowledge of all types that exist at this time due to the continual additions through history. The individual human being is a part of the larger team called humanity. The individual learns the lesson that giving it everything they have got in this life is an event that coincides with the attainment of the awareness of unconditional Love. When the entire team or humanity learns this same lesson then humanity is successful.

As giving maximum effort equals the awareness of the absolute power of Love, there is the gaining of such knowledge, which is then added to the knowledge that has emerged through history. This knowledge is used by every other human and leaders now and into the future. One observes that all of humanity is coming to the awareness of Love.

The combined evolutionary steps of individual men, women and children and the broader evolution of humanity as a whole will inevitably reach that point where each will, simultaneously, become totally evolved and enlightened. As more and more people on Earth are becoming spiritually aware, the time is coming closer and closer to the completion of the creation of a Heaven on Earth.

For this reason people alive right now have every reason be very hopeful and very optimistic about our future. Can you see how this is all coming together according to some, unseen plan?

There are times when one must face the doubts and uncertainties that arise. Those who believe that the human race is creating a new world based on the highest spiritual awareness are human beings, no better and no worse than any other. As all people have desires and doubts there are those times where one has to face the reality of the size of the endeavor. At this point there is the recognition that one must find the true source of faith and belief.

There is that inevitable point in every life where the choice must be made between Love and fear. This decision point is one of the ultimate destinations for every soul that resides in the body. What are the factors that can be identified when making this ultimate decision? The most important factor has to do with the awareness of that most feared day when we die.

When one understands and is totally aware of the inevitable destination of that day of transition then there is a complete change of perspective. The thoughts that we have change as we are cognizant of that day of soul movement. There is a rising of intensity concerning the whole set of beliefs that we hold and the strong desire to hold the absolute truth in our hands.

Love is a sacred reserve of energy; it is like the blood of spiritual evolution. –Pierre Teilhard de Chardin

B. Love is a sacred reserve of energy..

This writer believes that unconditional Love is present in every human being, every animal and everything on this Earth. This is the absolute truth that many hold in their hands right now. Is it possible that there are even more profound absolute truths that will be grasped as our souls evolve further? This is a question that will be answered at a certain point along our eternal journey.

We would say that the recognition of the fact that all of creation is existent because of unconditional Love, when that recognition is in all people, will without a doubt transform life on planet Earth. The process of spiritual evolution leading to the point where all have this recognition has been occurring since time began. The human race is very near to complete enlightenment through the recognition of unconditional Love.

As this increasing awareness moves on continuously through time one comes to understand that there is no turning back. When a man, woman or child thinks on the idea of unconditional Love and feels its immense power in the process, these thoughts and feelings cannot be unlearned or unfelt. After such recognition a human being is changed forever. This is the reaching of a stage that is part of the inevitable awakening process of every soul.

Every soul will come to this point or stage of spiritual evolution sooner or later. At the point of contact with unconditional Love the soul has the free will to hold onto unconditional Love and service to others or to hold onto those thoughts that have to do with ego and fear. The evolution of the human race as a whole sees more and more individuals coming to take the free will choice of unconditional Love and service to others over ego and service to self.

There is the recognition by the writer that he is writing these words with a certain amount of ego gratification involved. One would be less than honest without mentioning this fact. As the writer is a human being he faces the same ego/spirit issues that we all do. It is our hope that the words in this work will be free from any traces of ego gratification. We would hope that this work comes as close as possible to being sourced in unconditional Love.

If the writer is criticized or belittled for the work that is ok. This writing is meant to share the good news of the availability, to every man and woman and child on Earth, of unconditional Love. We state what we believe in an honest way so the chips will fall where they may. We are the athletes leaving it all on the field who accept no less than one hundred percent effort. Perhaps we have an unconscious wish to go down in history or receive a Nobel Prize for Peace.

We will be honest and say that we would not mind if the reading of these words came to such a point that proceeds from the sales allowed the writer total freedom to work for a world of unconditional Love.

Perhaps the readers will sense a certain amount of ego displayed by the writer in the words. We would like you to be certain that there is a conscious effort to stay away from ego in this work. We apologize if this effort is less than completely accurate at times. We are all human after all. Megalomania is defined as a psychopathological condition characterized by delusional fantasies of wealth, power or omnipotence. Any tinge of megalomania is hopefully absent and we hope this condition is not sensed by readers or is the source of any of these words.

Now the writer takes the risk of being seen as a megalomaniac for his fantasy of omnipotent power over the negative effects of megalomania. Can one have a perfect communication where there is no doubt that the ideas and thoughts conveyed are honest and free from ego or megalomania when one proposes the creation of Heaven on Earth; where all people grasp the power of unconditional Love?

Can the writer express the ideas and thoughts in such a way that anyone who takes in the concepts is aware that the effort is a genuine, honest one that truly represents the spirit of unconditional Love and forgiveness?

Come what may the work continues. The idea that those who are trying to create a new world of Love, peace, forgiveness and equality suffer from delusions of grandeur and megalomania are over. Now the expression of millions of people all over the Earth is that the creation of a new and better world, a new way of cooperating on Earth is entirely possible.

The views of millions and even billions of people on Earth of the potentials that are reachable in the area of human, spiritual evolution are no longer seen as wishful thinking or airy-fairy. Those who hold the belief that it is not possible to eliminate war, greed, hate and separation because that is 'the way life is' have the opportunity always to grasp the absolute power of Love. Unconditional Love, because it is unconditional, allows all to find their own way without condition.

There is a profound sense and knowing that this generation is creating a movement of such power and magnificence that the building of a Heavenly realm on Earth is going to really happen. God bless all who think on these things and create the environment where the thoughts of Heaven on Earth will result in its becoming a reality. We are making the observation that as more people think about a new world, the energy of this thinking is a real energy that pushes the ball toward the new human reality on this planet.

At a certain point the energy of collective human thinking becomes unstoppable and the manifestations of this powerful energy are seen in reality. This manifestation of a new world based on Love will be the most magnificent series of events that the human race has ever witnessed. It is going to happen and there is nothing that anyone, anywhere can do to stop it. The series of events that culminates in the literal manifestation of Heaven on Earth cannot be stopped because the power of unconditional Love is the only power in the universe.

This is how life works and how it shall be.

For us who are alive in the world at this time we are so fortunate to be able to witness these events with our eyes. We are trying to share the good news that this is the real situation. This new world is being created by millions and billions of people right now. This is happening as the truth of events that have occurred, and are occurring, through humanity's history is known by an increasing number of the people on Earth. Coinciding with humanity's grasp of the truth behind the events that have caused the suffering of humanity, there is a grasp of the truths surrounding spiritual matters.

The awakening of humanity is truly a magnificent thing to see. After so many centuries of wars, greed, poverty, starvation and inequality, people are coming to the conclusion that there is a better way to run this Earth. That better way is to base every action and thought on Love. This includes the actions that are taken by individuals and collectively as nations and humanity. Humanity has deemed that it is time for a change.

Some who will read these words will think that the idea of a new world based on Love is too good to be true. Consider the one who changes as a person from one who may be violent physically and mentally to one who has come upon Love. After this person discovers Love there is no longer a chance that he/she will harm any other. This person has in effect created their new world based on Love.

The only difference between the individual's transformation and humanity's transformation is scale. Logic tells us that if an individual can achieve spiritual transformation and that humanity is comprised of individuals then it is possible that humanity can be spiritually transformed. In fact humanity is being spiritually transformed at this moment.

We are who we have been waiting for.

This writer is no better and no worse than any other human being. We would like to help others in such a way that the realization of a new world is expedited. We are happy to join with men, women and children from around the Earth in this effort. To be included in this group of peacemakers is an honor and a privilege. We are willing to contribute in any way to eliminate suffering in this world.

It gives us all hope and optimism to know that there are increasing numbers of people who are joining the group that proclaims Love. If not now, when? Should humanity wait for a more opportune time to begin working for trust, cooperation and sharing between all people? There is no better time to begin than right now. Some will think that we have elected leaders to take care of this. We are saying that thinking about a new world of unconditional Love is important by itself. Many will ask: 'What can I do to help with such a massive effort?' All you have to do to contribute to the creation of a new world is to think about Love and then practice Love.

"A day spent without the sight or sound of beauty, the contemplation of mystery, or the search for truth or perfection is a poverty-stricken day; and a succession of such days is fatal to human life." –Lewis Mumford

II. Being Human.

A. A day spent without...

It just occurred to the writer that he may have bitten off more than he can chew. Just imagine yourself in the writer's shoes here. We are attempting to dream and bring into reality what many feel is an impossible dream. As a writer is one who shares his or her thoughts with the world, he or she tries to organize those thoughts for clear communication to anyone who reads the words.

When one considers the vision of a world where Love is the basis for every action there is a profound sense of responsibility felt. There is an accompanying concern that there is nothing but the honest sharing of thoughts conveyed which match the sizable vision. We feel that the vision is worthwhile to pursue so that will bring us the needed energy to dare the attempt.

If one could feel the feeling of a new world and all that it entails perhaps that feeling could aid greatly the effort to create such a world. Perhaps imagining what such a world will look like will be of help with the effort. Can we imagine this Earth without wars? How about seeing this world without greed and inequality? Is it possible to put an end to poverty and starvation?

"The power of Love, as the basis of a State, has never been tried... There will always be a government of force where men are selfish..." –Ralph Waldo Emerson

Perhaps if we can identify the causes of wars, greed, poverty, starvation and the rest of humanity's problems, then the solution of unconditional Love will become clear. Emerson seemed to indicate that selfish actions were responsible. We would concur. It is amazing to see the effects of advertising where people have actually based their own worth as a human being on how much they have compared to others.

Then the related amazement that people judge others by what they possess in the way of money and material things. This is seen by the ways that people interact with different people according to their possession of money or material things. We see people polite and respectful of the millionaire while ignoring the presence of the one who has nothing, looking down upon such a one with disdain. In reality there is no difference between people whatsoever.

Can we comprehend the true meaning behind the passage: 'It is easier for a camel to go through the eye of a needle than for a rich man to go to Heaven.'? This seems to be a very profound passage. Don't get us wrong here. We have nothing against people who achieve financial success. It seems that the passage points to those who become successful financially and forget about their fellow man. Can we imagine the lifestyles of those who have accumulated tremendous amounts of money and forgotten about their brothers and sisters in the family of man?

The presidential election just concluded in America and over two billion dollars were spent by the candidates. The President of the United States makes a salary of $400,000. This is worth taking some time to consider.

What would have been the result if those two billion dollars were redirected from political advertising to the aid of suffering people? The amount of people who are suffering from hunger and starvation could have been decreased substantially.

Why is money still a factor in elections? Without getting into a detailed analysis of the election system and the influence of money, why is money not simply removed from the elections of leaders? It seems perfectly clear that the election of a leader should be based on ideas alone.

Can we imagine a world where money is no longer considered important to the perceived value of a human being? We are envisioning that world where everyone is respected because they are a human being. This is the family of man where everyone is equal and respected. This describes the new world where there is no longer manipulation of geopolitical events to increase wealth for a few at the loss of the many.

Being human involves seeing and experiencing events and conditions on Earth which encompass the entire range of human emotions. We see and experience joyful events such as the miracle of birth, celebrations of Love at weddings and the end of wars. We also see and experience painful events such as the loss of a child at birth, divorce and the starting of wars.

In between are those emotional events and conditions which are of varying combinations of joy and pain. This is what it is to be human. The sum total of all of our experiences and witnessing equals a lifetime. It is absolutely fantastic to consider everything we as humans experience. There seem to be times in all of our lives where we come to take things for granted and under-appreciate the miracles that are everywhere.

The word miracle is defined as an extraordinary event manifesting divine intervention in human affairs. We remember watching the documentary, "The Miracle of Life" a few years ago on PBS. It was an episode of the science series Nova that focused on the human reproductive process from conception to birth. The movie records the whole process for the first time and absolutely should be required viewing for every high school student.

The movie is one of the most outstanding this writer has ever seen. The reason that we feel that the film should be shown to every high school student is that the true knowledge of human reproduction would eliminate youth pregnancies with their negative consequences. Our suggestion would be the requirement that every boy and girl in the eighth grade view this important movie. Not only would youth pregnancies come to a halt but those who view this movie will instantly receive true wisdom about the life process.

There will be a diminishment of disrespectful sexual conduct and those who partake in anything less than a high level of behavior will be seen as an outcast. This movie will result in the instantaneous awareness of the sacred value of life to every boy and girl who views it. Anyone who reads these words and is involved in the field of education is strongly urged to take the time to view "The Miracle of Life" and then do whatever you can to make it required viewing for every eighth grader in America and around the world.

It is that powerful of a film and would do nothing but good for every student. Many parents have a difficult time explaining the human reproductive process to their sons and daughters. This 1983 film achieves this explanation completely and magnificently.

So life begins for all living things at conception/birth and this in itself is truly a miracle. Can we imagine the supreme power and creative omnipotence of the force that made life and reality? One could say that from the birth of every living thing to the death of every living thing everything is a miracle.

"There are two ways to live: you can live as if nothing is a miracle; you can live as if everything is a miracle." – Albert Einstein

Albert Einstein really put his finger on it with that statement. When we live as if everything is a miracle we understand that everything is an extraordinary event of divine intervention in the affairs of humans. In other words everything that is visible is of the divine or God, including humans, animals, plants, stones… Everything is God.

As writers are considered wordsmiths the discussion now has run into a bit of difficulty as the topic of God, Creator, Allah, Great Spirit is somewhat hard to articulate. How does one explain the concept of deity or a supreme being? The highest spiritual realms will be experienced when we all cross over the great divide to the other side. Those who have had the near death experience have given us wonderful glimpses of a spiritual realm that human language has no words for.

The world is a sacred place and a sacred process; we are part of it. There are those who have attained spiritual knowledge to the point where they are able to experience astounding levels of mind and spirit. For example those who have spent much time in the practice of meditation describe states of blissful peace and an ability to see future events.

There is no need to compare your spiritual progress to anyone else. We all have our own paths to travel and it is not speed that counts. It is sincerity and good intent that matter. Be a good person is all. After all, to have compassion for others does not mean that you exclude compassion for yourself.

B. A Miraculous Course...

A Course in Miracles is a self-help course on spiritual thought that was scribed by psychologist Dr. Helen Schucman over a seven year period between 1965 and 1972. She obtained the information from an inner voice who many believe to have been Jesus Christ.

This writer finds that the messages in the course are some of the most profound he has ever come upon.

We will share our thoughts on passages from A Course in Miracles.

We are now going to take a journey into our inner worlds.

All learning is a help or hindrance to Heaven. You but chose whether to go towards Heaven, or away to nowhere. –A Course in Miracles (ACIM)

This seems to say that one should be discerning in their choice of learning avenues. An example would be the choice to read books that are glorifying violence or greed or less than Loving behavior. This choice is not one that will add knowledge that propels the person to Heaven. Instead the person is hindered or delayed from Heaven and spends unnecessary time on the path that leads to nowhere.

Perhaps a person spends time learning how to profit at the expense of others in a way that harms other people. There is the decision made to use manipulation of others for gain without concern for the welfare of those who are manipulated. This is seen in the world when people are lied to in order to manipulate events and actions. Those who consciously choose such behavior only hurt themselves in the long run as nothing is hidden in the world of spirit.

At this time in human history people all over Earth are making the choice to go towards Heaven. This is a result of a rising awareness and consciousness of the negative consequences experienced through history that come from choosing to go nowhere.

There is nothing else to choose.--ACIM

There are only these two options for individual humans and humanity as a whole. Every choice that we make moves us toward Heaven or away to nowhere. We are living in the time that has been predicted by the prophets where the return to spiritual wisdom and Love is chosen, felt and understood by all. Humanity has come to learn of the true realities on Earth and has come to the conclusion that the choice to move toward Heaven is now the correct choice.

With the tremendous increase in communication between people all over Earth comes learning and knowledge of the Earthly situations we are experiencing. This learning has been a help to humanity on its evolutionary path toward a Heavenly realm being created on Earth. As people become aware of those actions and activities that harm human beings they come to a knowing that the continuation of harmful actions and activities is leading nowhere.

Forgive the past and let it go, for it is gone. You have gone on, and reached the world that lies at Heaven's gate. –ACIM

Just as we all have done things in our lives that we are regretful of doing we need to forgive ourselves. As we understand that those actions which harmed others were wrong we grow toward that higher wisdom and move ahead. Because we understand the difference between the choice to harm and not to harm we have progressed and forgiving ourselves is called for. Apologize to those you have harmed if possible.

Forgive also those who have harmed you. You now understand that nobody in their right mind would intentionally harm another. Your forgiveness allows the other to see their better self and results in the discontinuance of their actions which hurt others and their own self. Now both can arrive at Heaven's gate where Love for others and oneself is understood. Forgiveness is essential for the health and well being of all.

Jesus forgave those who killed him.

Look gently on each other, and behold the world in which perception of hate has been transformed into a world of Love. –ACIM

We are seeing this occur in the individual lives of people with improved personal relationships among friends, family members and strangers. The increased understanding of the brotherhood and sisterhood of the family of man is leading humanity to the inevitable creation of a world fueled by and for Love. It is a tremendous thing to see this spiritual evolution occurring.

If everyone you meet is your brother or sister it is impossible to hate. This understanding eliminates any chance that hate will be perceived. Men and women will now look gently on each other with Love for their brother and sister. This transformation of perceptions on Earth is the greatest spiritual transformation that has ever been seen.

God's answer is eternal, though it operates in time, where it is needed. But, because it is of God, the laws of time do not affect its workings.

Unconditional Love, forgiveness and compassion are forever available to every human being. At any moment a person can experience unconditional Love for another person, animals or plants. This choice is there at each and every turn and it is up to the individual person whether that choice is taken or not. Whether we have decided to chose Love or not the opportunity to do so is eternally there for us. Now would seem to be a good time to choose Love.

Many are choosing Love now. This is what we are witness to at this time. There is no doubt that humanity is choosing Love and that in the near future people will be in a state of awe and reverence because of this choice. The manifestations of Love in the physical Earthly reality will be of such an intensity and power that all will be overwhelmed with joy and gratitude.

It is in this world, but not a part of it. For it is real, and dwells where all reality must be.

Reality is defined as the quality or state of being actual or true. Unconditional Love dwells in the heart of every man, woman and child on Earth. In other words every man, woman and child on Earth has absolute truth available inside of them. The kingdom of Heaven is within. This is the dwelling called Heaven and is described by those who have had a near death experience. These men and women describe being more real there than back here on Earth.

We are visitors here on Earth. We will return to our eternal homes when we transition back to spirit. Our purpose is to remember who we truly are and to help in some way to bring all to this remembrance. If our bodies are destroyed or not destroyed in the effort, our souls will go on into eternity. This leads us to the words of Jesus when he said: "Greater Love hath no man than this, that one lay down his life for his friends."

We have all had Loved ones pass on to the spirit world. Does it matter what age we attain in this life when eighty years is compared to eternity? We do not know when we will pass to spirit so can we do all in our power to leave a better, more Loving world to the future generations of humanity? The answer is yes and that is what we are witnessing on this Earth right now.

Forgiveness is the only function here, and serves to bring the joy this world denies to every aspect of God's son where sin was thought to rule.

Forgive yourself and forgive everyone for everything. Jesus forgave those who killed him. This eliminates all of the negative emotions which result from not forgiving. Anger, resentment, bitterness and ill will all harm your mental, physical and spiritual health. If Jesus could forgive those who killed him it is ridiculous of us to not find it in us to forgive someone for saying something stupid.

Jesus said: "Forgive them Father, for they know not what they do." See how your telling that person that you forgive them will result in improved communication and increase in joy for everyone concerned. This is a choice that can be made and will make all the difference in the world. Do not forget to apologize if you have descended into negative words or actions that hurt another. Cultivate sincerity

Forgiveness takes away what stands between your brother and yourself.

Can we see how forgiveness eliminates all of those differences that cause separation between human beings? How could we decide not to forgive? How could it be seen that non-forgiveness is the higher choice given all of the negative effects resulting from that choice? Simply to compare the choice of non-forgiveness to the choice of forgiveness makes it impossible not to become aware of the obvious positive consequences of forgiving.

An essential aspect of the ongoing creation of Heaven on Earth will be the complete understanding of the power of forgiveness. As many have the feeling that hanging the wrong-doers is called for, it is important to understand that those who committed the errors do not know what they have done. It is always possible for those who have erred, as we all have, to change in a good way.

God wills you learn what has always been true, that he created you as part of him, and this must be true because ideas leave not their source.

Is it possible that we, as eternal souls, all volunteered to come into this physical realm with the purpose of together creating a new, enlightened world? Would an examination of this possible reality of our purpose find that the creation of Heaven on Earth would be in alignment with God's will? One would be less than honest if they said that there has never been a time when they were concerned about the situation on Earth.

Any person who watches the news and sees human suffering exhibits that quality inherent in every human being that wants to do something to stop such suffering. This quality of wanting to stop suffering is proof that God created humanity as part of him. We are truly, each and every one of us, created by and are part of God.

In every wish to hurt he chooses death, instead of what God wills for him.

We are directed to the reports of those who have had a near death experience where they have viewed their life review. As these men, women and children viewed the movie of their life they would feel the hurt experienced by those they had hurt. At those points they are literally in the shoes of the other and feel what that other felt at that time.

It is astounding to realize that such a process as the life review exists in actuality and we will all have that experience. Those who come back from their near death experience and share the experience with us are sharing sacred knowledge. Can we see how when we choose to hurt others that we are choosing death instead of what God wills for us? Can we envision going through our life review and those points in our lives where we were either hurtful or Loving to others?

To use the power God has given you as he would have it used is natural. The gift of God to you is limitless.

The power that God has given all of us is witnessed in the world as humanity's actions to create a new and better Earthly reality. This is not any supernatural feat but the natural outcome of humanity's use of the limitless power of unconditional Love given to us by God. Humanity has glimpsed the limitlessness of the power of unconditional Love. With only a glimpse of awareness human beings have made tremendous positive contributions to the betterment of mankind. Can we imagine how much will be accomplished when humanity sees how limitless is the power of Love?

The power of Love is unlimited, infinite and inexhaustible. This is God's gift to every single man, woman and child in this world. The awareness of this fact is flooding the planet Earth at this time and is resulting in the most magnificent series of events that humanity has ever created. Consider how very fortunate you are to be alive at this time to witness these magnificent events.

Let us unite in bringing blessing to the world of sin and death. For what can save one of us, can save us all.

A blessing is defined as something promoting or contributing to happiness, well-being or prosperity. As one comes to understand the good changes in their life as a result of making the decision to accept the wisdom of Love, compassion and service to others there is the movement toward Heaven. When we interact with others with Love, forgiveness and compassion those others are then aware of the blessings of such a perspective.

One can then see how this awareness moves across the landscape of the Earth from heart to heart to heart to heart, bestowing blessing to the entire world. This is occurring now. It is just a matter of a short time until these blessings are felt by every man, woman and child in this world. At that magnificent moment the entire human race will be united and saved.

There is no difference among the sons of God.

Every man or woman you have known, met or will meet is equal in the eyes of the Creator. When one comes to the realization that every person has equally great worth there is no longer any illusion of separation between people. It does not matter if the person is rich, poor, healthy, sick, famous or unknown; all are treated with the same respect as sons and daughters of God.

This understanding removes all separation and the result is unity and oneness where it is impossible to harm others. There is the true knowing that when we harm another that we are harming ourselves. No longer will people look upon others as lower or higher in societies. We will see no more royalty or bluebloods that deserve adoration as a higher and more important group of humans.

Those who achieve fame and fortune will be seen as no different from those who suffer poverty, homelessness and starvation.

And yet to bless but one gives blessing to them all as one, your ancient name belongs to everyone, as theirs to you.

Can you see how the way you treat every single person you meet or interact with makes a difference in this world? When you give Loving service to others in the form of kind words and actions you are literally changing the world. This does not mean that one is to become a Pollyanna. Pollyanna is defined as a person who is regarded as foolishly or blindly optimistic. We are describing a person who is wisely and clear-sightedly optimistic.

Never hesitate to help others in any way. You are changing the world when you smile at someone, say a kind word, lend help to others who have need of assistance or take any action or thought with a benevolent intent. We do not know how far into every direction that the good consequences of our positive actions will travel and be felt. Give it a try soon and feel the difference.

Salvation is immediate. Salvation would wipe out the space you see between you still, and let you become as one.

Salvation is defined as deliverance or preservation from destruction, difficulty or evil. Can we see how spiritual wisdom leads us to salvation? We preserve ourselves from the destructive consequences of harmful words and actions such as wars or domestic violence. We deliver ourselves from the negative consequences of strained relations with members of our family or co-workers or friends.

All of those actions and thoughts that are based on separation would be wiped out and the deliverance from destructive, difficult consequences associated with these actions would occur. As soon as one thinks from oneness and not separation the immediate salvation is manifested in reality. Cooperation and understanding are then the guides for now and into the future.

And it is here you fear the loss would be, for a miracle is now. Be not content with future happiness.

If not now, when? How many have waited until they were on their deathbed to realize that they were ignorant of so many opportunities for happiness? These are those who wish that they had the chance to go back and live their lives in a different way that recognized the power of Love. There is no loss when you decide to live your life based on unconditional Love and forgiveness but only miracles.

Across this planet people are working toward the miraculous transformation of this world. Those who work for this most miraculous event in human history are not content with future happiness. There is no difference between your decision to smile at the checkout girl in the supermarket and humanity's decision to create a Heaven on Earth. Both you and all of humanity have made the decision to be happy now.

The Holy Spirit's purpose now is yours. Should not his happiness be yours as well?

There need be no living a life of quiet desperation when one chooses to live with unconditional Love for others and one's self. This choice allows you to spread joy to others and the whole world. This must bring you and others happiness. It is the way of happiness. There is a misconception surrounding spirituality that if one chooses to become more spiritual that then there must be solemnity and self denial.

Let us correct this misconception now and forever. Through the grasping and use of unconditional Love a person finds an increase in levels of joy and happiness. Remember that you choose to go toward Heaven or you choose to go nowhere. Choosing Heaven results in supreme joy, happiness and that peace which passeth all understanding.

What has been blocked is opened, what was held apart from light is given up, that light may shine upon it, and leave no space or distance lingering between the light of Heaven and the world.

The tremendous communication between people all over the Earth has opened up the potentials of humanity for all to see. As folks from every country and land on the planet discuss the issues of the day solutions are presented which are ready for consideration. Because of this increase in possible solutions being shared by people all around the world there is light being shined on potential solutions. Whereas before the communication revolution people had no way to express sensible solutions to the rest of the world's people, now this is happening and the world's people are becoming fully informed of the Earthly realities.

As human beings are inherently good and Loving the solutions are good and Loving as well. Now we see how the space or distance between the light of Heaven and the world is disappearing. The light of Heaven is shining upon the Earth. This condition allows for the new world of Heaven on Earth to be created.

The holiest of all the spots on Earth is where an ancient hatred has become a present Love.

The new world will see humanity viewing the entire Earth as holy. Through the power of unconditional Love and forgiveness every spot on planet Earth will be transformed to a Heavenly state where hatreds are overcome with Love. Those whose ancestors fought wars will recognize that these ancient hatreds were caused by errors in judgment by those ancestors and will be seen as in the past.

Those ancestors will be forgiven as all agree that the time has arrived for Love to be the basis for living. The evolutionary progress of humanity will be understood and accepted as the new realities come into existence. All sides will be in agreement and the good changes will become permanent with concern for future generations of humanity.

Your footprints lighten up the world, for where you walk forgiveness goes with you.

As all people come to understand the errors of the past and present as actions which simply need wisdom to correct, forgiveness will become a way of life that will increase humanity's wisdom tremendously. The world will become a lighter place with elimination of errors bringing peace to the entire Earth. The illusory dramas at every level of interaction from the personal to governmental and worldly will end.

The world will lighten up with Love and good feelings being shared everywhere, at all times. Forgiveness is now in the mind of every person and practiced as a part of the new ways of living on this planet Earth.

Where stood a cross stands now the risen Christ, and ancient scars are healed within his sight.

Humanity and the Earth have come back to life from the dead and are resurrected. This is the new world where all are reborn without memory of ancient error. Forgiveness is given to those who did not know what they were doing and the past and present are restored to health and soundness and repaired.

All are in agreement that this is the way that life shall be now and forever. There is no turning back to the past and human error. Humanity has firmly decided to forge the present and future in the good way.

In gentle gratitude to God the father and the son return to what is theirs, and will forever be.

Now is the Holy Spirit's purpose done. For they have come! They have come at last!

C. In gentle gratitude to God…

When a person finds within their mind that place where they meet Jesus Christ and connect with God it is the event that has been long awaited. Leading up to this event has been the living in the illusory world of the ego. Every person has the ability to choose to listen to their ego or to listen to the teaching of the Holy Spirit and Jesus.

The Holy Spirit's purpose is done when the person decides that the ego's lies are no longer wanted. Making the choice of living with ego as our teacher means that we will be experiencing guilt, anger, shame, pain and judgment. At a certain point we understand that there has to be a better way. Using the mind we come to choose again. We choose to deny the denial of truth and realize that the body is not real, the mind is real.

Their presence is obscured by any veil which stands between their shining innocence and your awareness it is your own, and equally belongs to every living thing along with you.

The presence of the Holy Spirit and Jesus Christ can be seen and felt when we come to eliminate the last traces of the ego. Our egos lie and tell us that we are separate from our Creator; that we are separate and different from others. The truth is that we were never separate from our Creator. We have simply put up a veil that hides this truth. Now we remove the veils of the ego and understand that we are all the same mind that is one with the Creator.

We have the power to defeat the ego and choose the right teacher. When this is done we can create peace, harmony and brotherhood in both our individual lives and those we touch. We understand that we have chosen the ego as our teacher and now we do not want this world of guilt and misery but decide to choose another thought system that reflects the Love of God.

God limits not, and what is limited cannot be Heaven, so it must be hell.

Forgiveness is the miracle that allows people the understanding that we are all the same and that we are one in Christ. Failure to forgive yourself or others results in feelings of guilt, blame, anger and despair. When we do not forgive ourselves we feel that we do not deserve happiness. We punish ourselves in order to please the illusory vengeful God that the ego has created.

We blame other people and the conditions in the world for our unhappiness and despair as we project outward our feelings of guilt. This is the hellish limitation of following the ego. When one chooses to listen to the Holy Spirit and Christ as teachers the ego is gone along with the hellish limitations. We now choose the unlimited, Heavenly mind of God, unconditional Love and forgiveness.

You have no enemy except yourself, and you are enemy indeed to him, because you do not know him as yourself.

As we use our minds erroneously to chose the ego over the Holy Spirit and Christ we hurt ourselves. We do not understand that we can choose again at any moment and that our salvation is immediate. This is possible for every person and it is simply about choice. Our magically insane mind comes to believe that we can punish ourselves so that God does not have to. This is a defense against what we really fear which is another thought system that is Love. We fear that we will lose ourselves and all that we have that separates us from other people and God.

The ego must be looked at and overcome to come to that place where we know who we really are. We are part of God and one in Christ. What you are will tell you of itself.

The Holy Spirit's purpose is to let the presence of your Holy guests be known to you.

The writer has to say that going over these passages from A Course in Miracles is a profound experience. We have read the text and find that the words are of that type where the meaning is intensified at each successive reading. This passage is striking in that one is astonished to learn that God and Christ are in each of us. Then to understand that their presence can be known to us is equally astonishing.

The writer is a human being like everyone else and this information has the same impact on him that it has on others. As we go over these passages the writer is thinking out loud so to speak. The information is somewhat abstract and we hope that you are lenient when considering our interpretations. We are afraid that our interpretations may miss the mark, where we may not precisely put our finger on the most articulate estimate of the message of the words.

Perhaps your interpretation of the words contained in these passages will be more in line than ours with the spiritual truth behind those words. If this be the case God bless you.

If you perceive injustice anywhere, you need but say, "By this do I deny the presence of the Father and the son, and I would rather know of them than see injustice, which their presence shines away."

Perhaps this passage calls for people who see an injustice to take an action which articulates how the presence of God and Christ in us should be acknowledged by those who have the power to stop the injustice. Maybe when we see injustice we are to move in such a way that the injustice is fully realized as the breaking of sacred spiritual law.

One recalls the time when Jesus entered the temple and overturned the tables of the moneychangers. He saw the injustice of the moneychangers taking advantage of the poor and had no choice but to take action. Perhaps we need to take action when we see an injustice instead of doing nothing or thinking that someone else can do something about it. Could the presence of God and Jesus in us shine away injustice?

Show this unto your brother, who will see that every scar is healed, and every tear is wiped away in laughter and Love.

This passage could be referring to any of a number of life situations where there is an injustice that is shined away. Perhaps a person is being treated unfairly because they are mentally challenged by those who feel that doing so will somehow raise them up in importance. When someone steps in to stop the unfair, hurtful treatment the person who was the recipient of the abuse is relieved, healed of the damage and feels joy that they have a friend.

Another situation could be your simple saying of the words, "I forgive you" to someone who is sincerely regretful of an action they took towards you.

Perhaps someone took the action of defending him in order to end the injustice. As the defender articulated the spiritual laws that have been broken with the injustice, God and Christ were seen by all involved. This led not only to the correction of the injustice but true understanding being gained by all those who were present.

Every scar created by the injustice and the denial of the presence of God and Christ were healed in all present. The tears created by the injustice and the tears created by the denial of the presence of God and Christ were transformed into true understanding and brotherhood.

And he will look on his forgiveness there, and with healed eyes will look beyond it, to the innocence that he beholds in you.

After reading these words one saw the image of scenes in a movie to portray such a powerful transformative experience. When we forgive others and they are aware that we have forgiven them, the emotions that are felt represent the presence of God and Christ. This feeling of the unseen by both you and the person you forgive is powerful for both.

The act of forgiveness raises the level of thought by all to a higher plane where God and Christ, unconditional Love and compassion are truly seen and felt in life changing ways. Can we imagine what this world will be like when the importance of forgiveness is grasped by all people?

Forgiveness is not real unless it brings a healing to your brother and yourself.

Can we recall all of those petty arguments we have been involved in through our lives? Petty is defined as of small importance or trivial. Looking back on these ridiculous dramas it is hoped that all involved were aware at some point just how meaningless they were. There have been reports of people seriously hurting others for small, trivial reasons. Any attempt to explain the how and why of these phenomena is almost futile.

One has to believe that it is learned behavior. Certainly ego is a major ingredient. Once the ego is defeated and forgiveness is fully appreciated such petty disagreements will disappear. When the writer learned of the near death experience and the life review that those who had the experience shared, he tried to apologize to everyone he had ever hurt. The life review finds the person experiencing what the other felt. If he/she hurt someone else they felt the pain of the other.

Upon learning this aspect of the life review the writer decided that apologies were in order. The act of forgiveness must be done in such a way that there is a true communication of that forgiveness.

Thus does the miracle undo all things the world attests can never be undone.

The miracle of forgiveness is such that all of the negative consequences of non-forgiveness are erased as if they never existed. Resentment, guilt, hatred, vengeance and anger are obliterated by forgiveness. The world or ego holds on to resentment, anger and plans for revenge as a way of blaming others for feelings of despair and depression. Forgiveness is not on the agenda of the ego.

This is why people should be aware of the workings of ego. The choice of ego as a teacher over God and Christ causes all of the anxiety, stress and negative emotions that a person suffers. We can see how the choice of God and Christ as teacher will eliminate all of these negatives through forgiveness. When all people understand this then the negative consequences of this world will be undone.

And hopelessness and death must disappear before the ancient clarion call of life.

Forgiveness is a life affirming act that gives hope and healing to all those who experience or witness it. This includes the person who forgives, the one who is forgiven and all those who witness the powerful transformative act.

All of the negative actions and consequences are eliminated through forgiveness and gives hope to mankind for a better world moving away from nowhere and death, toward Heaven and abundant life.

The ancient calling of the Father to his son, and of the son unto his own, will yet be the last trumpet that the world will ever hear.

Brother, there is no death.

We are not bodies with a soul but souls with a body. As we are a part of God and God is eternal this means that we are eternal. Eternal is defined as without beginning or end. When one is aware of this then everything changes. The profound nature of life is intensified and more greatly appreciated. The awareness that everyone one meets is also eternal is an astounding revelation.

Once there is this revelation there is no unlearning it. There is an intensified curiosity that is manifested as we are gripped by the desire to know the truth of our existence. The mundane events of our lives are no longer mundane. Life begins to take on an extraordinary quality where the sense is developed that this life is very important. We search for our purpose and destiny.

Death is a motivator of the highest order. One is overcome by a sense of the need to not wait to accomplish goals. Many of the greatest accomplishments in human history have been by those who have used death as an adviser, so to speak. What would happen if everyone lived each day as if it were their last one on Earth?

And this you learn when you but wish to show your brother that you had no hurt of him. He thinks your blood is on his hands, and so he stands condemned.

We let our brother know that we forgive him, wish them no harm and that we have no desire to give them a death sentence. He thinks he is guilty and deserves to be condemned to death but your forgiveness lets him know that there is no death. All this is the movement toward Heaven and away from nowhere.

But it is given you to show him, by your healing, that his guilt is but the fabric of a senseless dream.

You are giving your brother the understanding that there is another choice that he can make. He can choose to give up the ego and elect to adopt a thought system that expresses the Love of God. The ego is the senseless dream.

In quietness are all things answered, and every problem is quietly resolved. In conflict there can be no answer and no resolution.

Many spiritual traditions recommend the silence of meditation in order to find wisdom and peace. Perhaps when one senses an outbreak of conflict the best choice is silence. We can all recall regret for words spoken in haste that we wish were never said. It may be a good habit to cultivate patience before speaking so that the correct words are spoken.

Many learned spiritual men and women suggest the positive results of finding quiet time every day. Surely the spending of time in quietness for answers to problems is favorable to wasting time in conflict where there is no possibility of answers or resolutions.

The only way to heal is to be healed. The miracle extends without your help, but you are needed that it can begin.

Until one defeats ego, forgives oneself and accepts a new thought system based on God's Love they are not healed. When one takes these steps and is healed then that person becomes the source for the miraculous that heals others and extends out to others in an endless manner.

This is the miraculous we see occurring on Earth with the millions of people being healed with Love and Love's extension to every corner of the world. Thanks to the great ability of people to spread the healing message of Love this extension is occurring with blazing speed. The healing is rapid and many more are beginning the extension of Love to the point where its extension has become tremendous and is engulfing the world.

Accept the miracle of healing, and it will go forth because of what it is. It is its nature to extend itself the instant it is born.

When we forgive others and they are aware of our forgiveness then they will also forgive others. Once we begin this process with an act of forgiveness it extends in every direction endlessly. This writer cannot explain how this extension works but believes firmly that it does.

It is probable that forgiveness is inherently associated with absolute truth and unconditional Love. For this reason the magnificent power of the act, a spiritual power that is unseen, is indestructible and unstoppable.

The only thing that is required for a healing is a lack of fear. There is no sadness where a miracle has come to heal.

It is said that there are but two emotions and those are Love and fear. As humans we are operating from one or the other of these emotions at all times. There are no other options regarding human emotions. The lack of fear that is required for a healing means that we are coming from Love. And when we are coming from Love there is joy not sadness.

When we choose to come from Love we are the source of joy and healing for others. When this joy and healing is given to others they as well give it to others and so on it goes into forever.

And nothing more than just one instant of your Love without attack is necessary, that all this occur.

Just one instant of your Love without attack... How simple and easy it is to create the miraculous in this world. One need not read a millions books on religion, spirituality or theology. One need not look to the external world for this wisdom. This wisdom is built into every man, woman and child on Earth. Now we know what Jesus was talking about when he said: 'The kingdom of God is within you.'

Give an instant of your Love without attack to another and notice how you feel. How far will that instant of your Love without attack extend on this Earth?

Life is given you, to give the dying world.

Can you see how you are being given life to give to the dying world? Your actions make all the difference in the world. You may give someone who has contemplated suicide the renewed will to go on and share the gift you have given them. This person could go on and save the lives of others. Do you see how we are all connected this way?

You may move another in such a way that that person goes on to end a war. Perhaps that person will get in touch with a person who is famous and can move many to actions that are positive for humanity. Perhaps you will produce a work of art that moves others profoundly where you can then share your motivations of Love, forgiveness and compassion for all living things.

The holy instant's radiance will light your eyes, and give them sight to see beyond all suffering, and see Christ's face instead.

You are now seeing the Christ that is in all people including yourself. This is the reality of life that has been unknown until now. When this awareness is gained there is no way to see life the same as it was before. Everything has changed now and forever. When this awareness is known in all corners of the world there is no doubt that a new world is on its way.

You will now see every person in their real state of sacred value. No more will there be judging of people according to any illusory difference. When Jesus said that we must remember that what we do to the least among us we do to him, we now understand what he meant.

Thus is your healing everything the world requires, that it may be healed.

When you are healed the process of the entire world's healing begins. Your spiritual transformation is seen by others and the transformation becomes contagious. When all on the planet Earth are healed this is describing the second coming told of by the prophets.

Death shall be no more, neither shall there be mourning nor crying nor pain any more, for the former things have passed away.

It needs one lesson that has been perfectly learned. And then, when you forget it, will the world remind you gently of what you have taught.

We will forget the lesson of healing but never for long as the lesson is everywhere to see in the world. It is impossible not to learn this lesson of healing. Sooner or later, according to our choices, we will arrive at unconditional Love, forgiveness and compassion.

And happily your brother will perceive the many friends he thought were enemies.

D. And happily your brother will perceive...

Gone from your brother will be his insane thoughts of the ego. He will understand that God and Christ dwell in him and everyone. Those he thought were conspiring against him will be seen by him as the same as he is and as friends.

Peace be to you whom healing is offered. And you will learn that peace is given you, when you accept the healing for yourself.

The gift we receive when we accept the miracle of forgiveness is peace and the end of suffering. The gift we give to those we forgive is their peace and the end of their suffering.

What occurred within the instant which Love entered in without attack will stay with you forever.

The miracle of Love being shared is of such tremendous power that it is unforgettable. The forgiving moment is unforgettable for its power of spirit. Those who experience these things cannot forget them for all the days of their lives.

Yet all the witnesses you behold will be far less than all there really are.

This explains the extension of Love and forgiveness far beyond where the sharing took place. This passage reinforces the power of your good actions when interacting with others. You will remember those single instances of interacting with others but will be astonished when you learn how many witnesses there really are.

God thanks you for your healing, for he knows it is a gift of Love unto his son, and therefore is given to him.

When you forgive others you are healing both them and yourself; you are giving Love to others and yourself at the same time. Also at the same time you are doing God's will.

As fear is witness unto death, so is the miracle the witness unto life. The miracle forgives because it stands for what is beyond forgiveness, and is true.

As we mentioned earlier there are two human emotions: Love and fear. It is our choice to come from fear or Love at all times. As fear is associated with death and Love is associated with life it would seem to be an easy choice. It is an easy choice when we understand the consequences of both choices.

But there is need that you be healed, because the suffering of the world has made it deaf to its salvation and deliverance.

This describes the seeming lack of solutions to problems that contain the words Love and forgiveness. Do you watch the talking heads on television and notice that there is never any mention of the word Love in their intellectual discussions?

We now find more and more people being healed and this is the reason we are witnessing the magnificent spiritual awakening of humanity.

The resurrection of the world awaits your healing and your happiness, that you may demonstrate the healing of the world. What better function could you serve than this?

Resurrection is defined as the act of rising from the dead or returning to life. As people become healed the world is brought back to life and healed. These are very special times that we are living in. We are going to see the world healed.

He cannot doubt his dream's reality because he does not see the part he plays in making them, and making them seem real.

With our minds we choose the ego's lies over the truth of God and Christ. So we create the nightmarish dreams of the ego and believe that they are real.

The choice is yours to make between a sleeping death and dreams of evil, or a happy wakening and joy of life.

A Course in Miracles is a self-study spiritual thought system. There is a choice that can be made between the ego and the Holy Spirit that has negative or positive consequences depending on the choice that we make.

Rest in the Holy Spirit, and allow his gentle dreams to take the place of those you dreamed in terror and in fear of death.

The choice to use our minds in the thought system that expresses God's Love is the easy choice as it results in gentle dreams instead of the ego's nightmares.

Dream your brother's kindnesses instead of dwelling in your dreams on his mistakes.

Always seeing the best in others allows us to experience the joy of life in that we are sharing joy with others instead of thinking negatively about others. As we have all made mistakes in our lives realize that you have kindnesses and so do others. Forgive others and choose to live in joy instead of fear and mistrust.

Let all your brother's gifts be seen in light of charity and kindness offered you. And let no pain disturb your dream of deep appreciation for his gifts to you.

What this passage points to is the honoring of other people for their generosity and kindness at all times. Many times gifts are given and the receiver starts to think that the person giving has an ulterior motive and is not genuinely charitable and kind. We are to honor these noble traits in others with a deep appreciation.

The secret of salvation is but this: that you are doing this unto yourself. No matter what the form of attack, this is still true.

Let us consider the way that Jesus reacted to those who tormented and killed him. He forgave them. It is at all times our option to choose the path that leads to peace, Love and forgiveness.

Whatever seems to be the cause of pain and suffering you feel, this is still true. For you would not react at all to figures in a dream you knew that you were dreaming.

Because we have chosen the insane dreams of the ego we cause problems for ourselves and others. We have chosen to live by the ego and this finds us fearful of other people instead of Loving. We can change this by choosing again.

Let them be as hateful and vicious as they may, they could have no effect on you, unless you failed to recognize it is your dream. This single lesson will set you free from all suffering, whatever form it takes.

We find examples through history of those who were treated hatefully and viciously yet recognized it was their dream. The highest example is Christ. How astounding was this man's life story. To be willing to have your body killed while experiencing hate and scorn of an unimaginable level of intensity is such a display of unconditional Love.

As mentioned previously Jesus then forgives those who take his body and life.

The Holy Spirit will repeat this one inclusive lesson of deliverance, until it has been learned, regardless of the form of suffering that brings you pain.

We are responsible for creating our reality and the experiences that we have. There is nowhere to look but inside to end any suffering and pain that we create. It is the lesson that is impossible not to learn no matter how long it takes. Whether learned now or much later it will be learned.

And you will understand that miracles reflect the simple statement, "I have done this thing, and it is this that I will undo."

This understanding could be described as being born again. A new perspective has been developed and our actions and thoughts reflect this new perspective. Any mistakes that we have made will be repaired and corrected. Our actions will be taken based on the new perspective with the elimination of all errors.

Remember nothing that you have taught yourself, for you were badly taught. Who would keep a senseless lesson in his mind, when he can learn and can preserve a better one?

What we have a need to forget are the lessons of our egos which have taught us separation from God and others. This is the resurrection and being born again to the higher way of thought that corresponds to the Love of God.

What you remember never was. The miracle reminds you of a cause forever present, perfectly untouched by time and interference, never changed from what it is.

Until the time we are reborn what we know and remember is illusory and transient. The definition of transient is a passing especially quickly into and out of existence. When we choose unconditional Love and forgiveness we are choosing that which is eternal, changeless and forever.

And you are its effects, as changeless and perfect as itself.

Here we bump up against the erroneous thought that we are born as sinners. Nothing could be further from the truth. All one has to do is look into the eyes of a baby to know that we are all born of Love and are perfect in the eyes of God. That innocence is present in us at all times no matter the circumstance.

The miracle comes quietly into the mind that stops an instant, and is still. It reaches gently from that quiet time, and the mind it healed in quiet, then to other minds to share its quietness.

This passage points to the practice of meditation as a healing process. There need be no strict guidelines to follow when stilling the mind. One does not require a guru of any type to learn how to become quiet and still one's mind. This is a God-given right of every person for healing.

And they will join in doing nothing to prevent its radiant extension back into the mind that caused all minds to be.

Stilling one's mind allows for communication with God the Creator. It can be seen as a form of prayer where we talk to the spiritual world of the mind of God. Meditation need not be stiff and confining but should be open, flowing and easy.

Born out of sharing, there can be no pause in time to cause the miracle delay in hastening to all unquiet minds, and bringing them an instant's stillness where the memory of God returns to them.

Here we are face to face with the efforts of all those who wish to help others and create A New Earth. These are the majority of people on Earth who wish for an end to suffering and a world of Love, peace and forgiveness. This world where the memory of God is known by all and where all have attained peace and quiet minds is being constructed as we speak.

How instantly the memory of God arises in the mind that has no fear to keep the memory away.

When we choose Love over fear there is the instantaneous remembrance and connection with that in us that is of God.

When one achieves quiet and stillness in the mind they come into contact with that part of them that is eternal. Those souls in the eternal realm are overcome with joy.

What better way to close the gap between illusions and reality than to allow the memory of God to flow across it, making it a bridge an instant will suffice to reach beyond?

Here we are literally travelling from the ego world of illusion to the Love based world of true reality. This crossing of the bridge from insanity to sanity is a healing of our minds which is of the highest order. This crossing requires but the blink of an eye; an instant.

For God has closed it with himself. He has built the bridge, and it is he who will transport his son across it.

It is God's will, and so it is your will, that you cross the bridge from illusions to reality.

Have no fear that he will fail in what he wills. Nor that you will be excluded from the will that is for you.

No longer will you hold onto the insane belief that God's will is not possible. God is all-powerful and omnipotent. There is no possibility that you will fail to be transported by God to a higher destination. God wants the salvation and deliverance of every soul without exception.

It is because he is God's son that he must also be a father, who creates as God created him.

It could be said that we are all co-creators with God. The simple act of kindness that we decide to share with another is an example of us co-creating with God. Any action or thought which helps our fellow man is a co-creation with God.

The circle of creation has no end. Its starting and its ending are the same. But, in itself, it holds the universe of all creation, without beginning and without an end.

Here we find the concept of eternity and the infinite nature of creation. Becoming aware that everyone is an eternal co-creator with God changes one's perspective in a very dramatic way. There is an elimination of fears when we know that there is no end to our lives but that our souls are eternal.

The miracle does not awaken you, but merely shows you who the dreamer is. Do you wish for dreams of healing, or for dreams of death?

As we are co-creators with God we are shown here once again that we are responsible for our thoughts and what we experience. It is our choice at all times to create and dream either our healing and move toward Heaven or our disease and movement to nowhere.

But, for this change in content of the dream, it must be realized that it is you who dreamed the dreaming that you do not like.

We must take full and complete responsibility for our thoughts and their creative power. When we change our thoughts to those which are positive and healing then our reality will change in a positive and healing way.

In dreams of murder and attack are you a victim, in a dying body slain. But, in forgiving dreams is no-one asked to be the victim or the sufferer.

Through the powerful act of forgiveness we shed all of the anger, resentment and guilt that cause us to suffer and believe we are a victim.

These are the happy dreams the miracle exchanges for your own.

Forgiveness offers us the opportunity to eliminate the negative consequences of holding onto anger and revenge with their health destroying effects. When we forgive our enemies we are opening up the real possibility of resolution of differences in a way that is beneficial for all concerned.

We will literally be creating happiness in this world by making these choices.

It does not ask that you make another; only that you see you made the one you would exchange for this. The miracle establishes you dream a dream, and that its content is not true. This is a crucial step in dealing with illusions.

Illusion is defined as an erroneous perception of reality. When we perceive reality from the ego we are being deceived by a false perception or belief. It is at all times within our power to change our perceptions and beliefs in order to move past the illusory.

No-one is afraid of them, when he perceives that he made them up. The fear was held in place because he did not see that he was the author of the dream, and not a figure in the dream.

Now we are unafraid to rid ourselves of illusions once and for all. We understand that we created the illusions that we have been carrying and that we have the ability to eliminate them.

The miracle returns the cause of fear to you who made it. The world is full of miracles. They are the dream's alternative, the choice to be the dreamer, rather than deny the active role in making up the dream.

Once again we are to take full responsibility for our creations.

The body is released, because the mind acknowledges, "This is not done to me, but I am doing this." And thus the mind is free to make another choice instead.

We see on planet Earth at this time more and more people acknowledging in this way and deciding to make another, higher choice of creating a new and better world.

Beginning here, salvation will proceed to change the course of every step in the descent to separation, until all the steps have been retraced, the ladder gone, and all the dreaming of the world undone.

No longer will humanity descend into the illusory world where there is separation from God and our fellow brothers and sisters in the one family of man. Humanity ascends to that realm where true reality exists into eternity and it is impossible ever again to descend.

Healing is the effect of minds that join, as sickness comes from minds that separate. Count, then, the silver miracles and golden dreams of happiness as all the treasures you would keep within the storehouse of the world.

The only thing of value that we can create in this world is the Love and forgiveness that we give to and receive from others. This understanding is now flooding the Earth, its people, all animal life and all of the creation. The healing of our Earth and our humanity and all things has begun.

The door is open, not to thieves, but to your starving brothers, who mistook for gold a shining pebble, and who stored away a heap of snow that shone like silver.

God leaves the door open for all people no matter their degree of separation from him or other human beings. It is God's will that all should ascend the ladder to that place where Love, forgiveness and unity shine for all eternity.

And what are you who live within the world, except a picture of the son of God in broken pieces, each concealed within a separate and uncertain bit of clay? Be not afraid, but let your world be lit with miracles.

Do not hesitate to take any action and think any thought that helps your fellow man. Many times we hear people say, 'What can one person do?' Never again underestimate your unlimited God-given power when it comes to making a real, miraculous difference in this world.

The door is open that all those may come who would no longer starve, and would enjoy the feast of plenty set before them there. This is a feast unlike indeed to those the dreaming of the world has shown.

The feast of plenty consists of all the Love and forgiveness that we give and receive from others. The feast is unlimited and everyone is invited to share the good feelings of joy and happiness and togetherness. There is nothing on the table that is of separation or strife or conflict.

For here, the more that anyone receives, the more is left for all the rest to share. The guests have brought unlimited supply with them. Here the lean years enter not, for time waits not upon this feast, which has no end. For Love has set its table in the space that seemed to keep your guests away from you.

Unconditional Love and forgiveness eternally exist in unlimited supply and are endless in expanse. Every human being has the ability to go through the always open door and partake in the feast of unlimited supply. This ability can be exercised at any moment between now and eternity.

There is a way of finding certainty right here and now. Refuse to be part of fearful dreams whatever form they take. Thus you separate the dreamer from the dream, and join with one, but let the other go.

Never again will you choose to dream dreams of the ego with its insane perspectives. You will choose Love and forgiveness, the happy dream instead, as it is your inherent right as a human being to do so.

It is his reality that is your brother, as is yours to him. Your mind and his are joined in brotherhood. Therefore release him, merely by your claim on brotherhood, and not on dreams of fear. The Holy Spirit is in both your minds, and he is one, because there is no gap that separates his oneness from itself.

This oneness is being experienced by more and more people on Earth and we will see universal brotherhood become a reality on this planet in the near future.

Your willingness to let illusions go is all the healer of God's son requires. He will place the miracle of healing where the seeds of sickness were and there will be no loss, but only gain.

When we agree to eliminate the ego's grip on our perceptions and choose the better way the natural outgrowth of that choice results in healing. This healing repairs all disease and is extremely positive for everyone concerned.

God is the alternate to fear. Where fear has gone, there Love must come, because there are but these alternatives. Where one appears, the other disappears. And which you share becomes the only one you have. You have the one you accept, because it is the only one you want. There is no compromise. You are yourself or an illusion.

E. God is the alternate to fear...

This passage points to a universal truth that is very important for humanity to collectively learn. And it is being learned by humanity. Every human being wants Love to be apparent all over this beautiful Earth. Because this is the want of humanity so shall it be.

When you come to the place where the branch in the road is quite apparent, you cannot go ahead, you must go one way or the other. It is only the first few steps along the right way that seem hard, because you have chosen, but you still think that you can go back and make the other choice. This is not so. A choice made with the power of Heaven to uphold it cannot be undone.

Once you have made the choice of Love over fear there is no turning back because it is the only correct choice. The pettiness of fear and the ego is no match to the absolutely overwhelming power of Love. What analogy can we use to show just how puny is the power of fear compared to the tremendously awesome, powerful force of Love and Heaven?

Your way is decided. There is nothing you will not be told, if you acknowledge this. The beautiful relationship you have with all your brothers is a part of you because it is a part of God himself.

We have just felt and come to the awareness that these passages are poetry directly from the Creator. As a writer we wish it were possible to create words like these that are so pure and honest and spiritually powerful. You would probably agree with our sentiment that expresses a humble gratitude to have come into contact with these extremely powerful passages.

It gives us great hope that there is an organization to the creation that is learnable by us and gives us such profound insight, knowledge and wisdom. Thank you God, Creator for all of the blessings that you give to us as human beings.

Are you not sick if you deny yourself your wholeness and your health, the source of help, the call to healing and the call to heal? Your savior waits for healing, and the world waits with him. Nor are you apart from it.

The health, peace and happiness that we seek are available at every moment and all we have to do is Love and forgive.

For healing will be one, or not at all, its oneness being where the healing lies. There is no middle ground, in any aspect of salvation. You accept it wholly, or accept it not. Either there is a gap between you and your brother, or you are as one.

The definition of accept is to receive (something offered), especially with gladness or approval. How could we refuse to accept salvation and a guarantee of health and a beautiful new life? Accept wholly the healing of God with gladness and approval. Close the gap between yourself and others and become one.

The winds will blow upon it (the house of faith), and the rain will beat against it, but with no effect. The world will wash away, and yet this house will stand forever, for its strength lies not within itself alone. It is an ark of safety, resting on God's promise, that his son is safe forever in himself.

When we accept God's healing we become one with everyone we meet and we are forever safe in the house of faith. This is true because the Creator/God has promised it. We all will die and our world will be washed away but the house built on faith in God's promise stands forever.

There is no time, no place, no state where God is absent. There is nothing to be feared.

We will all come to that place where the decisive battle between Love and fear is fought. Our prayer is that all will defeat fear and share with all others on Earth the joy, happiness and peace seen in Love's victory.

Here is the fear of God most plainly seen. For Love is treacherous to those who fear, since fear and hate can never be apart. No-one who hates but is afraid to Love, and therefore must be afraid of God. Certain it is he knows not what Love means.

Treacherous is defined as marked by betrayal of fidelity, confidence, or trust, perfidious. Perfidy is defined as deliberate breach of faith, calculated violation of trust, treacherous. This passage offers us a remarkable revelation into the psychology surrounding Love and fear.

Please know that the writer is sharing this journey with you. It feels like there is a magical quality surrounding the words in these passages. Our guess is that you the reader are sensing the same sort of feeling; that we are coming into contact with very important truth here.

There is the sense that one is arriving at a place of ultimate truth and decision.

He fears to Love and loves to hate, and so he thinks that Love is fearful; hate is Love. The fear of God!-The greatest obstacle that peace must flow across has not yet gone. The rest are past, but this one still remains to block your path, and makes the way to light seem dark and fearful, perilous and bleak.

The greatest obstacle to peace is now in front of us. This point we are at is where the decision is made that determines our futures and the future of the human race on this beautiful Earth.

You had decided that your brother is your enemy. Sometimes a friend, perhaps, provided that your separate interests made your friendship possible a little while. It is not Love that asks a sacrifice, but fear demands a sacrifice of Love, for in Love's presence fear cannot abide. For hate to be maintained, Love must be feared, and only sometimes present; sometimes gone.

Can we see how this wisdom applies to situations where violence and war break out? There are those periods of time where the fighting is halted and Love is present. Then the fighting and violence breaks the truce and Love is gone. Fear has led to the sacrifice of Love.

Thus is Love seen as treacherous, because it seems to come and go uncertainly, and offers no stability to you. You do not see how limited and weak is your allegiance, and how frequently you have demanded that it go away, and leave you quietly alone in 'peace'.

Allegiance is defined as loyalty or the obligation of loyalty, as to a nation, sovereign, or cause. The cause is Love and forgiveness. Loyal is defined as faithful to a person, ideal, custom, cause or duty. So our faith and loyalty comes and goes, diminishing the power of Love and forgiveness to affect our lives and the lives of others.

There is a shock that comes to those who learn that their savior is their enemy no more. There is a wariness that is aroused by learning that the body is not real. And there are overtones of seeming fear around the happy message 'God is Love'. Yet all that happens when the gap is gone is peace eternal. Nothing more than that, and nothing less.

Wary is defined as cautious of danger, carefully watching and guarding against deception, artifices, and dangers. The ego's plan is to convince us that the body is real and not the mind. So we question the message 'God is Love' and in the process forestall our acceptance of eternal peace.

Without the fear of God, what could induce you to abandon him? What trinkets or toys in the gap could serve to hold you back an instant from his Love? Would you allow the body to say 'no' to Heaven's calling, were you not afraid to find a loss of self in finding God? And can your self be lost by being found?

This passage makes us think about what we are doing that is holding us back from the acceptance of the gift of

95

Love from God. It is impossible to lose our self when we find our self.

Why would you not perceive it as release from suffering to learn that you are free? Why would you not acclaim the truth instead of looking on it as an enemy? Why does an easy path, so clearly marked it is impossible to lose the way, seem thorny, rough, and far too difficult for you to follow? Is it not because you see it as the road to hell, instead of looking on it as a simple way, without sacrifice or any loss, to find yourself in Heaven and in God?

Acclaim is defined as to praise enthusiastically and often publicly; applaud; to acknowledge or declare with enthusiastic approval. The passage is pointing out the obvious, common sense facts of the rightness of choosing to accept the truth.

Until you realize you give up nothing; until you understand there is no loss; you will have some regrets about the way you have chosen. And you will not see the many gains your choice has offered you. Why are you not rejoicing?

Rejoice is defined as to feel joyful; be delighted. The words are pointing us to the evidence that is in plain sight. Now we see before us the truth and there is the correct interpretation which results in feelings of joy.

You are free of pain and sickness, misery and loss, and all effects of hatred and attack. No more is pain your friend and guilt your god, and you should welcome the effects of Love.

These are the gains that we receive and we should be very grateful for the actual receipt of these gifts.

Whom you forgive is given power to forgive you your illusions. By your gift of freedom is it given unto you. Make way for Love you did not create, but which you can extend. On Earth this means forgive your brother, that the darkness may be lifted from your mind. When light has come to him through your forgiveness, he will not forget his savior, leaving him unsaved. For it was in your face he saw the light he would keep beside him, as he walks through darkness to everlasting light.

This passage points us to the awareness that we are all one in Christ. There is that light of Love in every man, woman and child on Earth that is real and can be experienced by all. When we share this Love its effects are real and profoundly transformative in their nature. We see how this light is flooding the planet and creating

The New Earth. Humanity is literally walking through history's darkness and into the everlasting, eternal light of Love.

This is the spark that shines within the dream; that you can help him waken, and be sure his waking eyes will rest upon you first, and in his glad salvation you are saved.

When we grasp and understand unconditional Love we have the ability to lift others to that place of eternal light. As we lift others up to Love we are lifted as well.

You cannot dream from some dreams and wake from some, for you are either sleeping or awake. And dreaming goes with only one of these. For every dream is but a dream of fear, no matter what the form it seems to take. The fear is seen within, without, or both. Or it can be disguised in pleasant form.

We are asleep when we are dreaming. Because we are asleep our dreams are dreams of fear even though they may seem pleasant. When we waken the fearful dreams are no longer.

The miracle were treacherous indeed if it allowed you still to be afraid, because you did not recognize the fear. You would not then be willing to awake, for which the miracle paves the way. Because he Loves the dreamer, not the dream, each dream becomes an offering of Love. For at its center is his Love for you, which lights whatever form it takes with Love.

Your choice of Love and forgiveness substitutes the dreams of fear with those dreams that are offerings of Love.

There is a place in you where this whole world has been forgotten, where no memory of sin and illusion linger still. The changelessness of Heaven is in you, so deep within that nothing in this world but passes by, unnoticed and unseen.

This is probably that place where those proficient in spiritual and meditative practices have developed an ability to go to. This ability is one that every human being has but not all have developed.

The still infinity of endless peace surrounds you gently in its soft embrace, so strong and quiet, tranquil in the might of its Creator, nothing can intrude upon the sacred son of God within. Nothing is asked of you but to accept the changeless and eternal that abide in him, for your identity is there.

In order to experience the endless peace that is inside of and available to you, all you have to do is accept it.

Every thought of Love that you offer him but brings you nearer to your wakening to peace eternal and endless joy. A dream is given you in which he is your savior, not your enemy in hate. Why does it seem so hard to share this dream? Because, unless the Holy Spirit gives the dream its function, it was made for hate, and will continue in death's services Such is the core of fear in every dream that has been kept apart from him who sees a different function for the dream..

When we do not allow the Holy Spirit into our thought system we will continue to suffer from dreams of hate and fear.

Forgiving dreams are means to step aside from dreaming of a world outside yourself, and leading finally beyond all dreams, unto the peace of everlasting life. You were not born to die. You cannot change, because your function has been fixed by God.

Function is defined as the action for which a person is particularly fitted or employed. Human beings all have a function that has been fixed by God and there is nothing we can do to change this. The sooner we accept this the sooner we will experience the travelling beyond dreams and arrival at the peace of everlasting life.

All other goals are set in time, and change that time might be preserved, excepting one. Forgiveness does not aim at keeping time, but at its ending, when it has no use. Its purpose ended, it is gone. And where it once held seeming sway is now restored the function God established for his son in full awareness.

We have come across some passages here where the concepts are somewhat abstract. The statement that forgiveness aims at ending time perhaps is pointing to the eternal nature of all of us with regard to our souls. One thinks of the concept of reincarnation where the soul becomes fully enlightened and no longer needs to reincarnate to learn the lessons which it has finally learned. Hence this soul is freed from the cycle of birth and rebirth and returns to God where there is no time.

This is the writer's interpretation. Yours may be different and/or more precisely explanatory.

Time can set no end to its fulfillment, nor its changelessness. There is no death, because the living share the function their Creator gave to them. Life's function cannot be to die. It must be life's extension, that it be forever and forever, without end.

These words seem to point at the meaning of our existence as human beings where enlightenment is inevitable for our souls whether it takes one lifetime (incarnation) or hundreds of lifetimes. The reincarnation process will never change as the Creator has fixed this function into every human soul. Either way we are forever beings.

This world will bind your feet and tie your hands and kill your body, only if you think that it was made to crucify God's son. For even though it was a dream of death, you need not let it stand for this to you. Let this but be changed, and nothing in the world but must be changed as well. For nothing here but is defined as what you see it for.

The ultimate example is the life of Jesus Christ. If this knowledge actually came through Dr. Helen Schucman from Christ we are on Holy ground here. Having this perspective, that these words are from the real Christ, gives us a sense of sacred wisdom being conveyed. Christ understood that his soul was forever so his perspective on death was not that it is a crucifixion but a resurrection. It is a returning, an ascending back, to our eternal home from whence our souls descended. This understanding changes everything.

How lovely is the world whose purpose is the forgiveness of God's son! How free from fear, how filled with blessing and happiness! And what a joyous thing it is to dwell a little while in such a happy place! Nor can it be forgotten, in such a world, it is a little while 'til timelessness comes quietly to take the place of time.

This passage points us to the absolute power of forgiveness and the overwhelmingly positive consequences of choosing to forgive. One also considers the brevity of each lifetime and the remembrance of the short amount of time before our souls return to spirit where there is no time, but timelessness.

Seek not outside yourself. For it will fail, and you will weep each time an idol falls. Heaven cannot be found where it is not, and there can be no peace excepting there. There is no other answer you can substitute, and find the happiness his answer brings. Seek not outside yourself.

This is the writer's first attempt at truly finding the meaning of these passages and we must say that the effort has produced some extremely powerful emotions. It seems that when one gives a serious look at the words that they are made of gold and are living, absolute truth.

As we have mentioned the writer is a human being like all of us, no better and no worse. This has been a tremendous journey into the literal truth of our existence, the true meaning of life. One feels a deep sense of humility and profound gratitude upon sharing this wisdom with others.

Be you glad that you are told where happiness abides, and seek no longer elsewhere. You will fail. The fear of God is but the fear of the loss of idols. Salvation thus appears to threaten life, and offer death. It is not so. Salvation seeks to prove there is no death, and only life exists. The sacrifice of death is nothing lost.

The writer is aware of a deep responsibility to convey to the reader nothing but the highest expression of thought here as the ground we are on is sacred ground. We want to let you know there is a concern that he will fail to convey thoughts to the reader in a way that is commensurate with the absolute power of the words we are witness to.

One feels like a reporter in the presence of God trying to give the audience the story of the event. There is the sense that this reporter has taken a reporting assignment that is so far above his ability and experience that someone made a mistake in the delegation of the assignment.

We will complete the assignment and the story will be delivered.

An idol cannot take the place of God. Let him remind you of his Love for you, and do not seek to drown his voice in chants of deep despair to idols of yourself. Seek not outside your father for your hope. For hope of happiness is not despair. What is an idol? Do you think you know? Idols are but substitutes for your reality.

This passage points us to the false belief that material things are what it is all about. Success is defined as the accumulation of money, cars, houses, clothing and more than our brother and sister. These are idols and nothing but substitutes for the unconditional Love that God has for every human being.

In some way you believe they will complete your little self, and let you walk safely in a world perceived as dangerous, with forces massed against your confidence and peace of mind. This is the penalty for looking not within for certainty, and for a quiet calm which liberates you from the world, and lets you stand apart in quiet and in peace unlimited. This world of idols is a veil across the face of Christ, because its purpose is to separate your brother from yourself.

As we worship idols we are unaware that every man, woman and child in this world share in the oneness of Christ. The separation we witness between people is caused by the worship of money and material things. As the veil across the face of Christ is being lifted at this time humanity is consciously removing the idea of separation and coming into the truth of our oneness.

This is the antichrist; the strange idea there is a power past omnipotence, a place beyond the infinite, a time transcending the eternal. Here does the changeless change, the peace of God, forever given to all living things, gives way to chaos. And the son of God, as perfect, sinless, and as Loving as his father, comes to hate a little while, to suffer pain, and finally die.

As we write these words there is chaos in the area of the Earth known as the Middle East. There is chaos in the economies, and the lives of citizens, in most countries

106

on the planet. This chaos is evidence that the veil across the face of Christ must be removed to allow the complete awareness by humanity of our oneness.

Where is an idol? Nowhere! The world believes in idols. Each worshipper of idols harbors hope that his special deities will give him more than other men possess. It must be 'more'. It does not really matter more of what, - more beauty, more intelligence, more wealth; or even more affliction and pain. An idol is a means for getting more. And it is this that is against God's will.

It strikes one as astonishing that we are witness to the world believing in idols. There is most definitely the effort by people to attain more possessions than others. Men and women go to the plastic surgeon for' more' beauty than others. Those with college educations and those with irrational estimates of intelligence, all those who have 'more' intelligence, condescend to and separate themselves from others with 'less' intelligence. Those who have more money and material things raise themselves up to show the world that they are 'more' than those who suffer with poverty.

God gave you all there is. And to be sure you could not lose it, did he also give the same to every living thing as well. No idol can establish you as more than God, but you will never be content with being less. The slave of idols is a willing slave, for willing he must be, to let himself bow down in worship to what has no life, and seek for power in the powerless.

Will we be able to take all of our 'more' with us when we transition from this life to the world of spirit and timelessness? Our bank account, houses, cars, clothing and jewelry mean nothing in that place. All that matters is what we did for our fellow man. All that matters is the Love and forgiveness we shared while alive in the body.

We will all make the transition to spirit.

While we are here will we worship the lifeless and look for spiritual power where it is not?

A dream of judgment came into the mind that God created perfect as himself. And in that dream was Heaven changed to hell, and God made enemy unto his son. Whenever you feel fear in any form, -and you are fearful if you do not feel a deep content, a certainty of help, a calm assurance Heaven goes with you, -be sure you made an idol, and believe it will betray you.

The definition of betray is to lead astray; especially: seduce. The definition of astray is defined as away from the correct path or direction. We can now look at the consequences of creating idols and the consequences of not creating idols. The creation of idols results in fear no matter what form. Not creating idols results in a deep content, a certainty of help and a calm assurance that Heaven goes with us.

Forgiving dreams remind you that you live in safety, and have not attacked yourself. Forgiving dreams are kind to everyone who figures in the dream. And so they bring the dreamer full release from dreams of fear. The first rule, then, is not coercion, but a simple statement of a simple fact. You will not make decisions by yourself whatever you decide. For they are made with idols or with God.

The definition of coerce is to force to act or think in a certain way by use of pressure, threats or intimidation. A simple statement of a simple fact says that we are free to decide whether we want God and the release of fear or idols and the continuance of fear in our lives.

These are the two options and there are no others.

And you ask for help of Christ or antichrist, and which you choose will join with you, and tell you what to do. Your day is not at random. There is no freedom from what must occur. And if you think there is, you must be wrong. Decisions cause results because they are not made in isolation. They are made by you and your advisor, for yourself, and for the world as well.

This passage points us to the fact that there is a decision that must be made and that the consequences of our decisions have real impact on ourselves and the entire world. There is that old saying about the point where the rubber meets the road. When we decide whether our advisor is Christ or antichrist what follows is reality experienced.

Do you not understand that to oppose the Holy Spirit is to fight yourself? God but ensured that you would never lose your will, when he gave you his perfect answer. Hear it now, that you may be reminded of his Love, and learn your will. He joins with you in willing you to be free.

It is both God's will and ours to Love and forgive. This points us to the meaning behind Christ's words when he said, 'You shall know the truth. And the truth shall set you free.'

And to oppose him is to make a choice against yourself and choose to be bound. Look once again upon your enemy, the one you chose to hate instead of Love. Now hear God speak to you through him who is his voice, and yours as well, reminding you that it is not your will to hate, and be a prisoner to fear, a slave to death, a little creature with a little life.

When we think again we understand that we want to Love and forgive and that this is God's will as well as our own.

Your will is boundless; it is not your will to be bound. What lies in you has joined with God himself in all Creation's birth. Remember him who has created you, and through you created everything. God turns to you to ask the world be saved, for by your own salvation is it healed. And no-one walks upon the Earth but must depend on your decision, that he learn death has no power over him because he shares your freedom, as he shares your will.

F. Your will is boundless...

The definition of boundless is being without boundaries or limits; infinite. When we make this ultimate decision we must be cognizant of the fact that every single human being on Earth depends on that decision. God gives us responsibility for the entire human race and the Creation.

It is your will to heal him, and because you have decided with him, he is healed. And now God is forgiven, for you chose to look upon your brother as your friend. The thought God holds of you is like a star, unchangeable in an eternal sky. So high in Heaven is it set that those outside of Heaven know not that it is there. But still and white and lovely will it shine through all eternity. Who knows the Father knows this light, for he is the eternal sky which holds it safe, forever lifted up and anchored sure. But those who seek for idols cannot know this star is there.

Decide to know that you are that unchangeable, eternal star which God sees you are. That place where your star is set so high in Heaven is reachable for every human being. Once reached by every man, woman and child the seeking of idols will end and the light of the stars of the human race will shine for all eternity.

Beyond all idols is the thought God holds of you. Surrounded by a stillness so complete no sound of battle comes remotely near. It rests in certainty and perfect peace. Here is your one reality kept safe, completely unaware of all the world that worships idols, and that knows not God. You have not two realities, but one. An idol or the thought God holds of you is your reality.

Once again we are given the choice of idols or the thought God holds of us.

Forget not, then, that idols must keep hidden what you are, not from the mind of God, but from your own. The star shines still; the sky has never changed. But you, the holy son of God himself, are unaware of your own reality. Reality observes the laws of God, and not the rules you set. It is his laws that guarantee you safety. All illusions that you believe about yourself obey no laws. They seem to dance a little while, according to the rules you set for them. But then they fall, and cannot rise again. They are but toys, my children. Do not grieve for them.

Here we learn that illusions are temporary toys that are doomed to fail. When we give our allegiances to idols and not the laws of God the reality of what we are is covered up in our minds. The illusions we create are there for a while but they are transitory, not the eternal and changeless wisdom of God. The sooner we let go of the illusions of ego and idols the sooner we arrive at who and what we truly are.

Appearances deceive because they are appearances, and not reality. Dwell not on them in any form. They but

114

obscure reality. And they bring fear because they hide the truth. God's son needs no defense against his dreams. His idols do not threaten him at all. His one mistake is that he thinks them real. And you can make a simple choice that will forever place you far beyond deception. You need not concern yourself with how this will be done, for this you cannot understand.

We have no ability to understand how the process of moving beyond the deception of appearances and illusions works but that is nothing to be concerned about. All we are asked is to make the simple choice to move beyond the illusions and it is done.

But you will understand that mighty changes have been quickly brought about, when you decide one very simple thing; you do not want whatever you believe an idol gives. For thus the son of God declares that he is free of idols. And thus he is free. No more than this is asked. Be glad indeed salvation asks so little, not so much. It asks for nothing in reality. And even in illusions it but asks forgiveness be the substitute for fear.

With one simple decision we are free and it is an act that requires so little to bring to our realities. All we need to do is forgive.

Such is the rule for happy dreams. The gap is emptied of the toys of fear, and then its unreality is plain. Dreams are for nothing. And the son of God can have no need of them. They offer him no single thing that he could ever want. He is delivered from illusions by his will, and but restored to what he is. What could God's plan for his salvation be, except a means to give him to himself? The real world is the state of mind in which the only purpose of the world is seen to be forgiveness.

Imagine the world where humanity understands that the only purpose of the world is forgiveness. What you are seeing in your mind's eye is The New Earth. This is The New Earth that is in the process of being created now. Every man, woman and child will be restored to what he or she is, back to their original condition as a perfect reflection of God.

The value of forgiveness is perceived, and takes the place of idols, which are sought no longer, for their 'gifts' are not held dear. Here it is thought that understanding is acquired by attack. There it is clear that by attack is understanding lost. The world becomes a place of hope, because its only purpose is to be a place where hope of happiness can be fulfilled.

Hope is defined as the feeling that what is wanted can be had or that events will turn out for the best. At this moment hope is filling the world with the anticipation of the best outcome where a new and better world comes into existence. Because of this increasing hope on planet Earth there will be the fulfillment of the feeling that what we want as humanity will occur.

And no-one stands outside this hope, because the world has been united in belief the purpose of the world is one which all must share, if hope be more than just a dream. Not yet is Heaven quite remembered. For the purpose of forgiveness still remains.

Heaven is not yet remembered because the state of Heaven on Earth is one where there is no longer any need for forgiveness. Every man, woman and child will need to be in that state of awareness where there are no more idols and no possibility of taking actions which forgiveness absolves.

Yet he is glad to wait till every hand is joined, and every heart made ready to rise and go with him. For thus is he made ready for the step in which is all forgiveness left behind. The final step is God's, because it is but God who could create a perfect son, and share his

117

fatherhood with him. No-one outside of Heaven knows how this can be. For understanding this is Heaven itself.

Is it possible that the hands of every man, woman and child can be joined and every heart made ready to rise and go with God? Can every beautiful soul on this beautiful Earth join together and allow God to take the final step where all forgiveness is left behind, no longer needed?

For he whose hand you hold was waiting but for you to join him. An ancient hate is passing from the world, and with it goes all hatred and fear. Look back no longer, for what lies ahead is all you ever wanted in your hearts. Give up the world! But not to sacrifice. You never wanted it.

We now understand that a better world of unconditional Love for all lies in front of us and is the only thing our hearts have desired. The illusions of history are disappearing along with all hatred and fear. There is no turning back.

What happiness have you sought here that did not bring you pain? Joy has no cost. It is your sacred right, and what you pay for is not happiness. Be merciful unto your brother, then. The will of God forever lies in those whose hands are joined. Until they joined, they thought he was their enemy. But when they joined and shared a purpose, they were free to learn their will is one. And thus the will of God must reach to their awareness. Nor can they forget for long that it is but their own.

As more and more people on Earth are joining hands there is the awareness that we are one in will and that this will is the will of God. The creation of a new and better world is humanity's will and the will of God.

Anger is never justified. Attack has no foundation. It is here escape from fear begins, and will be made complete. Here is the real world given in exchange for dreams of terror. For it is on this forgiveness rests, and it is but natural. Forgiveness recognized as merited will heal. It gives the miracle its strength to overlook illusions. This is how you learn that you must be forgiven too.

Anger and attack are actions that originate in the ego and terror-filled dreams of fear based on illusions. Forgiveness allows us to move past illusions when we are forgiven as well.

Look on your brother with the willingness to see him as he is. And do not keep a part of him outside your

119

willingness that he be healed. To heal is to make whole. Nor will you know him, if you think he does not merit the escape from guilt in all its forms and all its consequences. There is no way to think of him but this, if you would know the truth about yourself.

In order for us to know the truth about ourselves we need to also know the truth about others. How often do we make snap judgments about others without the willingness to see the others as they really are? When we are making those snap judgments do we have the willingness for the others to be healed? How often do we judge other people where we have made up our mind that the other is not deserving of the escape from guilt and the negative aspects of such guilt?

Appearances deceive but can be changed. Reality is changeless. It does not deceive at all. And if you fail to see beyond appearances, you are deceived. The miracle is means to demonstrate that all appearances change because they are appearances, and cannot have the changelessness reality entails.

Perhaps we could use an example to illustrate. Let us say that we have a friend who said something unkind to us. Perhaps he has had a hard week at work where there were some unfortunate events that he had to experience. So he vents on you because you are the only one around. Without your knowledge of his bad week you are deceived by appearances. Because you are aware that you value your friendship you will try to understand why we acted in such a way by seeing past appearances. You understand that he said these things not because of anything you did so you forgive him, and the appearance changes.

Because of this you have avoided being deceived by appearances and kept a friend.

The miracle attests salvation from appearances by showing they can change. What is temptation but a wish to make illusions real? There is no miracle you cannot have when you desire healing. But there is no miracle that can be given unless you want it. The Christ in him is perfect. Is it this you would look upon? Then let there be no dreams about him that you would prefer to seeing this.

When we see Christ in everyone our perceiving is correct as indeed the light of Christ is shared by all. So we should make it our habit to see the light in everyone.

And you will see the Christ in him because you let him come to you. And when he has appeared to you, you will be certain you are like him, for he is the changeless in your brother and you. Why should you fear to see the Christ in him? You but behold yourself in what you see. As he is healed are you made free of guilt, and his appearance is your own to you. Take heed then when you are called upon to fulfill your function as teachers that you teach the truth about God's son.

In these passages it is made very clear that Christ is shared by all of humanity. The awareness of this, which results in all people seeing the Christ in themselves and all others, is surely being gained by many more human beings every day. This bodes very well for humanity so look forward to the brightest of futures.

The only way that you can experience any peace while this unfortunate necessity for interpreting illusions remains is to recognize that you are discussing only illusions, and that this has no real meaning at all. Try to say a prayer for your brother while doing this and you will call forth and experience a miracle instead.

How simple is salvation! All it says is what was never true is not true now, and never will be. Only

unwillingness to learn it could make such an easy lesson
difficult. How hard is it to see that what is false cannot
be true, and what is true cannot be false? Why, then, do
you persist in learning not such simple things?

This passage is very straightforward and simple. Have
you ever experienced those times where you just could
not understand something that was so simple? Then
when you finally understood you feel like a fool because
you realize now that it was so simple all along.

There is a reason, but confuse it not with difficulty in the
simple things salvation asks you to learn. It teaches you
but the very obvious. The lessons you have taught
yourselves have been so over-learned and fixed they rise
like heavy curtains, to obscure the simple and obvious.

Could these words be reflected in the talking heads we
see on television who are the experts on the big
problems that humanity faces? You know, the men and
women who have advanced degrees from prestigious
universities who have read a million complex books in
their fields.

Could the lessons they have taught themselves have
been so over-learned that the heavy curtain obscures the
simple and obvious? When was the last time you heard

one of these experts in the area of warfare and violence say that the resolution is for all to recognize the Christ in all and Love and forgive?

Say not that you cannot learn them. You, who have taught yourselves the son of God is guilty, say not that you cannot learn the simple things salvation teaches you. Yet you will learn them, for their learning is the only purpose for your learning skill the Holy Spirit sees in all the world. His simple lessons in forgiveness have a power mightier than yours, because they call from God and from yourself to you.

The power of unconditional Love and forgiveness is greater than all of the advanced degrees because it is true reality and from God.

The outcome of the lesson that God's son is guiltless is a world in which there is no fear, and everything is lit with hope, and sparkles with a gentle friendliness. The soft, eternal calling of each part of God's creation to the whole is heard throughout the world this second lesson brings. Without your answer is it left to die, as it is saved from death when you have heard its calling as the ancient call to life, and understood that it is but your own.

The ancient call to life is inextricably tied to our own call to life. We are in the middle of everything in this world. What we decide is mirrored in the world in such a way that we are responsible for the events on the Earth. There is no separation between what goes on in our individual lives and the situations and events that are occurring on the planet.

We are to answer the soft, eternal calling of each part of God's creation to the whole or this calling will die.

God's perfect son remembers his creation. But in guilt he has forgotten what he really is. Be innocent of judgment, unaware of any thoughts of evil or good that ever crossed your mind of anyone. Now do you know him not. But you are free to learn of him, and learn of him anew. Now he is born again to you, and you are born again to him, without the past that sentenced him to die, and you with him. Now he is free to live, as you are free, because an ancient learning passed away, and left a place for truth to be reborn.

Because we have changed our perspective by following the simple lessons of the Holy Spirit fear and illusion have died and in its place truth is reborn.

Let us review again what seems to stand between you and the truth of what you are, for there are steps in its relinquishment. The first is a decision which you make. But afterwards, the truth is given you. Be very still for a moment. Nothing will hurt you in this holy place to which you come to listen silently, and learn the truth of what you really want. No more than this will you be asked to learn.

Relinquish is defined as to withdraw or retreat from: leave behind. So we are to leave behind what is blocking the path to the awareness of what we are as human beings. We must first be willing to enter the stillness and quiet.

But as you hear it, you will understand you need but come away without the thoughts you did not want, and that were never true. He asks and you receive, for you have come with but one purpose; that you both may learn you Love each other with a brother's Love. Together is your joint inheritance remembered and accepted by you both. Alone it is denied to both of you. For next to you is one who holds the light before you, so that every step is made in certainty and sureness of the road. And he who travels with you has the light.

126

Here we are meeting the Christ within. The definition of inherit is to come into possession of or receive especially as a right or divine portion. When we realize that we share the Love with and for Christ we accept and receive the divine inheritance of travelling with the light of Christ.

Learn this and learn it well, for it is here delay of happiness is shortened by a span of time you cannot realize. You never hate your brother for his 'sins', but only for your own. Are you sin? You answer 'yes' whenever you attack, for by attack do you assert that you are guilty, and must give as you deserve. Thus you think, within the narrow band from birth to death, a little time is given you to use for you alone; a time when everyone conflicts with you, but you can choose which road will lead you out of the conflict, and away from difficulties which concern you not.

The joining with Christ within us is the only sure and certain way to true happiness. This wisdom is essential to comprehend and master through experience and study.

But they are your concern. How, then, can you escape from them by leaving them behind? What must go with you, you will take with you whatever road you choose to walk along. Real choice is no illusion. But the world has none to offer. All its roads but lead to disappointment, nothingness and death. All of them will lead to death. On some you may travel gaily for a while, before the bleakness enters. And on some the thorns are felt at once. The choice is not what will the ending be, but when it comes.

G. But they are your concern...

Sooner or later we all will face the fact that the world has no answers to our inquiries about who we truly are.

Men have died on seeing this, because they saw no way except the pathways offered by the world. And, learning they led nowhere, lost their hope. And yet this was the time they could have learned their greatest lesson. All must reach this point, and go beyond it. The lesson has a purpose, and in this you come to understand what it is for. Learn now, without despair, there is no hope of answers in the world. Think not that happiness is ever found by following a road away from it. A journey from your self does not exist.

Will we wait to learn the lesson that the world's pathways lead to nowhere and death? Many are coming to learn this greatest lesson around the world and are participating in the greatest spiritual evolution the world has ever seen. Many more are reaching this point of great learning and moving beyond it now.

Where could it go? You cannot escape from what you are. For God is merciful, and did not let his son abandon him. For what he is be thankful, for in that is your escape from madness and death. Nowhere but where he is can you be found. There is no path that does not lead to him. You will make many concepts of the self as learning goes along. There will be some confusion every time there is a shift, but be you thankful that the learning of the world is loosening its grasp upon your mind.

Thank the Creator/God that you are learning that there is no separation between God, Christ, all other persons and yourself. This is the oneness behind the great New Earth that you are helping to bring into reality. We have escaped from the madness and death of the world and are on the journey to unconditional Love, forgiveness, the creation of Heaven on Earth and then eternity.

And be you sure and happy in the confidence that it will go at last, and leave your mind at peace. The role of the accuser will appear in many places and in many forms, and each will seem to be accusing you. But have no fear it will not be undone. There will come a time when images have all gone by, and you will see you know not what you are. There is no statement that the world is more afraid to hear than this: 'I do not know the thing I am, and therefore do not know what I am doing, where I am, or how to look upon the world and on myself'. Yet in this learning is salvation born. And what you are will tell you of itself.

Here we arrive at the place of highest importance regarding true perception.

You see the flesh or recognize the spirit. There is no compromise of the two. If one is real the other must be

130

false, for what is real denies its opposite. There is no choice in vision but this one. What you decide in this determines all you see, and think is real, and hold as true. On this choice does all your world depend, for here you have established what you are, as flesh or spirit in your own belief.

This is the point where the greatest choice a human being makes occurs. We have come to the place of decision that changes everything. Is our true reality the body or is it the mind and spirit? When we see ourselves as bodies we have decided upon fear, hate and death. When we understand that our true reality is our soul and spirit, Love and forgiveness, then we know that there is no death and that we are eternal.

If you choose flesh, you will never escape the body as your own reality, for you have chosen that you want it so. But choose the spirit, and all of Heaven bends to touch your eyes, and bless your holy sight, that you may see the world of flesh no more except to heal and comfort and bless. Salvation does not ask that you behold the spirit and perceive the body not. It merely asks that this should be your choice. It is your world salvation will undo, and let you see another world your eyes could never find. Be not concerned how this could ever be.

When we choose the spirit over the flesh we are given the ability to see with the eyes of spirit. In this physical realm we do not know how this occurs. All we know is that the world is not as it was before. Now we grasp unconditional Love and forgiveness and wish to heal, comfort and bless our brothers and sisters in the family of man.

The veil of ignorance is drawn across the evil and the good, and must be passed that both may disappear, so that perception finds no hiding place. How is this done? It is not done at all. What could there be within the universe that God created that must still be done? Only in arrogance could you conceive that you must make the way to Heaven plain. The means are given you by which to see the world that will replace the one you made.

In every human being there is the ability to see the Heavenly realm that will replace the hellish world that we have created. We need only choose spirit over flesh.

Your will be done! In Heaven as on Earth this is forever true. It matters not where you believe you are, or what you think the truth about yourself must really be. It makes no difference what you look upon, nor what you choose to feel or think or wish. For God himself hath said, 'Thy will be done' and it is done accordingly. One vision, clearly seen, that does not fit the picture as it was perceived before, will change the world for eyes that learn to see, because the concept of the self has changed.

The will of God and our will have come to be chosen and known by all as the same. We are now co-creators with God and we see the New Earth that is being created with unconditional Love and forgiveness. The New Earth will be created because humanity has a new concept of itself.

Are you invulnerable? Then the world is harmless in your sight. Do you forgive? Then is the world forgiving, for you have forgiven its trespasses. And so it looks on you with eyes that see as yours. Are you a body? So is all the world perceived as treacherous, and out to kill. Are you a spirit, deathless, and without the promise of corruption and the stain of sin upon you? So the world is seen as stable, fully worthy of your trust; a happy place to rest for a while, where nothing need be feared but only Loved.

When we accept that our true reality is that we are spirit, we know that we are eternal so nothing can harm us. We spend our days in this world by forgiving, sharing Love and joy, and trusting that Christ is in all without exception. The world that we see will change from a treacherous one to one where Love, forgiveness and happiness are evidence of spiritual wisdom.

Who is unwelcome to the kind in heart? And what could hurt the truly innocent? Thy will be done, you holy child of God. It does not matter whether you think you are in Earth or Heaven. What your father wills for you can never change. The truth in you remains as radiant as a star, as pure as light, as innocent as Love itself. And you are worthy that your will be done.

The eternal truth of God/Creator is inside of every human being without exception. As truth is inside of us our first understanding must be the correct direction in which to look. We have been told that the truth is outside of us so that is where we must focus our eyes. But the truth is within. There is that place inside of every man, woman and child where truth resides and can be reached. This place is unconditional Love.

Learning is change. Salvation does not seek to use a means as yet too alien to your thinking to be helpful, nor to make the kinds of change you could not recognize. You cannot give yourself your innocence, for you are too confused about yourself. But should one brother dawn upon your sight as wholly worthy of forgiveness, then your concept of yourself is wholly changed. And as you gave your trust to what is 'good' in him, you gave it to the 'good' in you.

The spiritual truth of our existence is inside of us all and it is understandable. We have the ability to understand the truth and change ourselves for the better along with the world around us. The most important aspect here is that we can feel the good change and recognize the power of forgiveness and unconditional Love.

And this will be your concept of yourself, when you have reached the world beyond the sight your eyes alone can offer you to see. For you will not interpret what you see without the aid that God has given you. And in his sight there is another world. Have faith in him who walks with you, so that your fearful concept of yourself may change. And all this shift requires is that you be willing that this happy change occur. No more than this is asked.

All that we are asked is to allow God's truth to enable the happy change in us. We then are able to see the world through the eyes of spirit with the help that God has given all of us without exception. Humanity is reaching the world beyond the sight its eyes alone can see. This world is The New Earth.

Hold out your hand, that you may have the gift of kind forgiveness, which you offer one whose need for it is just the same as yours. And let your cruel concept of yourself be changed to one which brings the peace of God. All that is given you is for release; the sight, the vision and the inner guide all lead you out of hell with those you Love beside you, and the universe with them. And to each one has he allowed the grace to be a savior to the holy ones especially entrusted to his care. And this he learns when first he looks upon one brother as he looks upon himself, and sees the mirror of himself in him.

When we understand the oneness of all things we can no longer see any separation between ourselves and others. How could we harm ourselves by harming our brothers and sisters or any living thing? Grace is defined as an unmerited divine assistance given humans for their regeneration and sanctification. Regeneration is defined as spiritual renewal or revival; rebirth. Sanctification is defined as to make holy; set apart as sacred; consecrate.

With God's grace we are led out of the hellish and into the world of oneness, unconditional Love and forgiveness.

And in this single vision does he see the face of Christ, and understands he looks on everyone as he beholds this one. For there is light where darkness was before, and now the veil is lifted from his sight. What is temptation but the wish to stay in hell and misery? Who has learned to see his brother not as this has saved himself, and thus is a savior to the rest. The holy ones whom God has given each of you to save are everyone you meet or look upon, not knowing who they are; all those you saw an instant and forgot, and those you knew a long while since, and those you will yet meet, the unremembered and the unborn.

H. And in this single vision…

Humanity will soon find itself in the position where all will see the face of Christ in all. Every man, woman and child will see through the eyes of spirit the true world of reality. From this present moment and into eternity life on the Earth will be seen truly through the eyes of God.

For God has given you his son to save from every concept that he ever held. For holiness is seen through holy eyes that look upon the innocence within, and thus expect to see it everywhere. This is the savior's vision; that he sees his innocence in all he looks upon, and sees his own salvation everywhere. For vision can but represent a wish, because it has no power to create. Yet it can look with Love or it can look with hate, depending only on the simple choice of whether you would join with what you see, or keep yourself apart and separate.

As the human race accepts unconditional Love and forgiveness, hate and guilt are vanishing from the face of the Earth. Every human being is changing their concept of themselves and seeing the holiness of all through the holy eyes given to us by God.

Be vigilant against temptation, then, remembering that it is but a wish, insane and meaningless, to make yourself a thing which you are not. It is a thing of madness, pain and death; a thing of treachery and black despair, of failing dreams and no remaining hope except to die, and end the dream of fear. This is temptation, nothing more than this. Be not deceived by what appear as many choices. There is hell or Heaven, and of these you choose but one.

Vigilant is defined as alertly watchful especially to avoid danger. Always choose Heaven. Always choose unconditional Love. Always choose forgiveness.

Let not the world's light, given unto you, be hidden from the world. Their savior stands, unknowing and unknown, beholding them with eyes unopened. And they cannot see until he looks on them with seeing eyes, and offers them forgiveness with his own. Can you to whom God says, 'Release my son!' be tempted not to listen, when you learn that it is you for whom he asks release? And what but this is what this course would teach? And what but this is there for you to learn?

This spiritual wisdom brings tears to your eyes. They are tears from the eyes that have opened to the seeing of forgiveness of the world and our own release in the process.

Temptation has one lesson it would teach, in all its forms, wherever it occurs. It would persuade the holy son of God he is a body, born in what must die, unable to escape its frailty, and bound by what it orders him to feel. Would you be this, if Christ appeared to you in all his glory, asking you but this, 'Choose once again if you would take your place among the saviors of the world, or would remain in hell, and behold your brothers there.' For he has come, and he is asking this.

We are now face to face with Christ in the moment of decision. We will each decide with our free will.

How do you make the choice? How easily is this explained! You always choose between your weakness and the strength of Christ in you. And what you choose is what you think is real. Trials are but lessons which you have failed to learn presented once again, so where you made faulty choice before you now can make a better one, and thus escape all pain which what you chose before has brought to you. In every difficulty, all distress, and each perplexity you face, Christ calls to you, and gently says, 'My brother, choose again.' He would remove all misery from you whom God created altars of joy.

The moments that make up a lifetime are filled with choice between our weakness and the strength of Christ which is in all of us without exception. We each have the ability to choose at every moment the strength of Christ.

He would not leave you comfortless, alone in dreams of hell, but would release your minds from everything that hides his face from you. His holiness is yours because he is the only power that is real in you. His strength is yours because he is the self that God created as his only son. The images that you make cannot prevail against what God himself would have you be. The saviors of the world, who see like him, are merely those who choose his strength instead of their own weakness seen apart from him. They will redeem the world, for they are joined to all the power of the will of God.

The definition of redeem is to recover ownership of by paying a specified sum. Through our choice of Christ's strength we are redeeming the world's ownership of our true reality by paying for it with unconditional Love and forgiveness.

And what they will is only what he wills. Learn, then, the happy habit of response to all temptation to perceive yourself as weak and miserable with these words: 'I am as God created me. His son can suffer nothing. And I am his son.' You are as God created you, and so is every

142

living thing you look upon, regardless of the images that you see. What you behold as sickness and as pain, and as weakness and as suffering and loss, is but temptation to perceive yourself defenseless and in hell.

Yield not to this, and you will see all pain in every form wherever it occurs but disappear as mists before the sun. Deny me not the little gift I ask, when in exchange I lay before your feet the peace of God, and the power to bring this peace to everyone who wanders in the world, uncertain, lonely, and in constant fear. For it is given you to join with him, and through the Christ in you unveil his eyes, and let him look upon the Christ in him.

I. Yield not to this...

The peace of God is at this time flooding the planet Earth and all of her inhabitants. Very soon all will see the Christ in themselves and that is in all others. All of us who have been lonely, fearful wanderers will have the peace of God that is shared by all.

My brothers in salvation, do not fail to hear my voice and listen to my words. I ask for nothing but your own release. There is no place for hell within a world whose loveliness can yet be so intense and so inclusive it is but a step from there to Heaven. To your tired eyes I bring a vision of a different world, so new and clean and fresh you will forget the pain and sorrow that you saw before. But this is a vision which you must share with everyone you see. For otherwise you will behold it not. To give this gift is how you make it yours.

The vision of a new and clean and fresh different world must be shared with everyone we see. When we give this gift of the vision of a new and different world then we own the vision and join with others in the continuing creation.

Humanity is creating a new world of such an intense beauty and oneness that we will be at the doorstep of Heaven.

And God ordained, in Loving kindness, that it be for you. Hear me, my brothers, hear and join with me. God has ordained that I cannot call in vain. And in his certainty I rest content. For you will hear, and you will choose again. And in this choice is everyone made free.

The vision of a new and clean and fresh world is one that God wants for humanity. This vision is being brought into reality on Earth as we speak. Every man, woman and child on Earth will soon be free.

I thank you, Father, for these holy ones who are my brothers as they are your sons. My faith in them is yours. I am as sure that they will come to me as you are sure of what they are, and will forever be. They will accept the gift I offer them because you gave it me on their behalf. And as I would but do your holy will, so will they choose. And I give thanks for them. Salvation's song will echo through the world with every choice they make. For we are one in purpose, and the end of hell is near.

Salvation is defined as preservation or deliverance from destruction, difficulty, or evil. Salvation's song will soon be heard in every part of this world as hell is replaced by a Heaven on Earth.

In joyous welcome is my hand outstretched to every brother who looks with fixed determination toward the light that shines beyond in perfect constancy. Give me my own, for they belong to you. And can you fail in what is but your will? I give you thanks for what my brothers are, and as each one elects to join with me, the song of thanks from Earth to Heaven grows from tiny, scattered threads of melody to one inclusive chorus from a world redeemed from hell, and giving thanks to you.

As humanity comes together as one there will be a worldwide chorus that will sing the song of thanks to God for the successful completion of his, and humanity's, will.

And now we say 'Amen': for Christ has come to dwell in the abode you set for him before time was, in calm eternity. The journey closes, ending at the place where it began. No trace of it remains, not one illusion is accorded faith, and not one spot of darkness still remains to hide the face of Christ from anyone.

Before we came into the physical realm we had already known that the joining with Christ was going to occur in our lifetime. We had a place in our spirit and soul for him to reside that was arranged for in eternity before we descended to the world of time. Now we have assented to the Christ living in our hearts. So be it.

Thy will is done, complete and perfectly, and all creation recognizes you and knows you as the only source it has. Clear in your likeness does the light shine forth from everything that lives and moves in you.

For we have reached where all of us are one, and we are home where you would have us be.

III. Unconditional Love.

I believe that unarmed truth and unconditional Love will have the final say in reality. –Martin Luther King (1929-1968)

Unarmed truth and unconditional Love will have the final say in reality. When Martin Luther King spoke these words he was delivering a prophecy of the future. We believe that this prophecy of Martin Luther King is being fulfilled at this time in human history. Prophecy is defined as an inspired utterance of a prophet, viewed as a revelation of divine will. Prophet is defined as a person who speaks by divine inspiration or as the interpreter through whom the will of God is expressed. Martin Luther King was a prophet.

Other prophets of God have predicted what is occurring at this time. We are witnessing the days of prophecy fulfilled. The human race is feeling this fulfillment either consciously or unconsciously. More and more people are coming to sense that the time we are in is extremely special as the will of God and the will of ourselves is being manifested in reality.

Love conquers all. –Virgil (70 B.C.-19 B.C.)

The Roman poet Virgil summed up life here with these three words. This simple statement describes humanity's state in the new world that is now being established. The New Earth is one where unconditional Love is going to be known and experienced by all people. The definition of conquer is to defeat or subdue by force. The absolute power of Love will defeat fear, hate separation and war.

If you could only Love enough, you could be the most powerful person in the world. –Emmet Fox (1886-1951)

Emmet Fox was trying here to articulate the power of Love. What he seems to be trying to say is that when we Love we are tapping into the most powerful force in the universe, and that the more we Love the more of that power is gained and absorbed by us. This is not to say that we are seeking after power over others or any such

150

thing. Fox was talking about the power of Love to help us solve and eliminate any problems that we are experiencing. He was coming from the concept of using the power of Love to heal ourselves along with others.

All my life, my heart has yearned for a thing I cannot name. –Andre Breton (1896-1966)

Human beings have tried to define Love since time began. Andre Breton is sharing a feeling that many have which shows us the somewhat indefinable quality of Love. Breton was one of the founders of Surrealism, a literary and artistic movement that attempts to express the workings of the subconscious. Breton here gives us another perspective on the definition of Love.

A Loving heart is the truest wisdom. –Charles Dickens (1812-1870)

Dickens is considered one of the greatest novelists who ever lived. Here Dickens distills his wisdom in a very simple, straightforward statement. Dickens' novels include David Copperfield, Oliver Twist, A Tale of Two Cities, Great Expectations and A Christmas Carol.

Time is short for those who wait, too swift for those who fear, too long for those who grieve, too short for those who rejoice, but for those who Love, time is eternity. – Henry Van Dyke (1852-1933)

Henry Van Dyke was an American author, educator and clergyman. In this quote Van Dyke points to the timeless quality that is experienced by those who Love. As Love is timeless, changeless and eternal when we Love we are sensing and feeling those qualities.

The one thing we can never get enough of is Love. And the one thing we never give enough is Love. –Henry Miller (1891-1980)

Henry Miller was a novelist most famous for writing, 'Tropic of Cancer' in the 1950's. He and Ernest Hemingway were considered the two most important novelists of their time. Miller here is pointing to the power of Love and how we as humans need to give and receive Love more often.

The moment you have in your heart this extraordinary thing called Love and feel the depth, the delight, the ecstasy of it, you will discover that for you the world is transformed. –Jiddu Krishnamurti (1895-1986)

Krishnamurti was an Indian born speaker and writer on philosophical and spiritual subjects. What he is talking about here is the new world that one experiences when Love is allowed into one's heart.

This personal transformation is no more and no less than the spiritual transformation of humanity which occurs when large numbers of people allow Love into their hearts.

You will find as you look back upon your life that the moments when you have truly lived are the moments when you have done things in the spirit of Love. –Henry Drummond (1851-1897)

Henry Drummond was a Scottish born evangelist, writer and lecturer. This statement shows Drummond's looking back on his life and the realization that true living is synonymous with being associated with the spirit of Love. He lived from 1851-1897.

Love is a force more formidable than any other. It is invisible-it cannot be seen or measured, yet it is powerful enough to transform you in a moment, and offer you more joy than any material possession could... Love's greatest gift is its ability to make everything it touches sacred. –Barbara De Angelis

Barbara De Angelis is an American relationship consultant, lecturer, writer and TV personality. Here she points out the power and force of Love and its ability to give us joy even though it is unseen and immeasurable. She compares the joy that is produced by material things and the greater joys that are experienced with Love.

She rightly points out Love's greatest gift which makes all those who Love aware of the sacredness of all things in the creation.

He is not a Lover who does not Love forever... Love is all we have; the only way that each can help the other. – Euripides (480 B.C.-406 B.C.)

Euripides was a Greek playwright whom Aristotle called the most tragic of the Greek poets. Euripides is saying that there is a difference between the Love that lasts a short while and the true Love that lasts into eternity. He comes to the conclusion that Love is all that humanity has which allows us to help each other.

Love is life. And if you miss Love, you miss life... Love is always bestowed as a gift-freely, willingly and without expectation. We don't Love to be Loved; we Love to Love... What Love we've given, we'll have forever. What Love we fail to give, will be lost for eternity. –Leo Buscaglia (1924-1998)

154

Leo Buscaglia lived from 1924-1998 and was known as 'Dr. Love'. He was an American author, lecturer and professor. His most famous book was 'Living, Loving and Learning'. Here Buscaglia speaks from the perspective of eternity; he is looking back from the hereafter world of spirit. He advises that human beings should concentrate on taking every opportunity to Love.

At the touch of Love everyone becomes a poet... Love is the joy of the good, the wonder of the wise, the amazement of the gods.—Plato (424 B.C.-347 B.C.)

Plato was a Classical Greek philosopher, mathematician, student of Socrates and writer of philosophical dialogues. He founded the Academy in Athens, one of the great philosophical schools of antiquity. Here Plato displays his deep understanding of the importance of Love in our lives.

It is not because things are difficult that we do not dare, it is because we do not dare that they are difficult... It is a rough road that leads to greatness... Love in its essence is spiritual fire. –Lucius Annaeus Seneca (4 B.C.-65 A.D.)

Lucius Annaeus Seneca was a Roman Stoic philosopher, statesman and playwright. Here Seneca gives his wisdom on accomplishment where the daring is the important first step in doing what may be considered difficult things. We could say that humanity, on its historical evolutionary path, has travelled the rough road to greatness. Now we see humanity achieving greatness through the use of Love; the spiritual fire.

To bear with patience wrongs done to oneself is a mark of perfection, but to bear with patience wrongs done to someone else is a mark of imperfection and even of actual sin... Love takes up where knowledge leaves off. –Thomas Aquinas (1224-1274)

Thomas Aquinas was one of the great philosophers and theologians. He says here that our standing by in the face of injustice is not an ideal way of living. He notes that after knowledge is deemed insufficient to solve problems then Love is capable.

When Love is at its best, one Loves so much that he cannot forget. –Helen Hunt Jackson (1830-1885)

Helen Hunt Jackson was a novelist, travel writer and essayist and one of the most successful authors and passionate intellects of her day. Ralph Waldo Emerson described her at the time as 'the greatest American woman poet'. Jackson shares her idea of the highest

Love where the people involved are unable to forget the moments. This is similar to the dramatic moment in a movie that is impossible to forget.

Nobody has ever measured, not even poets, how much the heart can hold. –Zelda Fitzgerald (1900-1948)

Zelda Fitzgerald was an American novelist and the wife of novelist F. Scott Fitzgerald. She is saying that there is perhaps an infinite capacity of the human heart to hold Love. This is a profound observation on her part as she points to the tremendous potentials that all human beings possess surrounding the concept of Love.

Who so Loves believes the impossible. –Elizabeth Barrett Browning (1806-1861)

Elizabeth Barrett Browning was one of the most prominent poets of the Victorian era. She lived from 1806-1861. The spirit of her quote can be transferred to the belief in the impossible creation of The New Earth. As an individual who Loves believes the impossible so when humanity creates a world that is based on unconditional Love and forgiveness, humanity believes the impossible.

We are all born for Love. It is the principle of existence, and its only end. –Benjamin Disraeli (1804-1881)

Benjamin Disraeli was Prime Minister of the United Kingdom on two separate occasions, first in 1868 and then between 1874 and 1880.

For Love is immortality. –Emily Dickinson (1830-1886)

Emily Dickinson lived from 1830 to 1886 and was a reclusive American poet. She is regarded as one of the great American poets and she never achieved success until after her death. Her words here are contained in a simple statement yet are profound in that they point to the eternal power of Love.

Sometimes it's a form of Love just to talk to somebody that you have nothing in common with and still be fascinated by their presence. –David Byrne

David Byrne was born in Scotland in 1952 and is now a resident of America. He is a musician best known for being a member of the group Talking Heads. He brings us down to Earth, so to speak, with his observation of the wide range of ways there are for us to experience Love.

There is always something left to Love. And if you ain't learned that, you ain't learned nothing. –Lorraine Hansberry (1930-1965)

Ms. Hansberry was an African-American playwright and author best known for 'Raisin in the Sun'.

Only divine Love bestows the keys of knowledge. – Arthur Rimbaud (1854-1891)

Rimbaud was a major French poet in the second half of the 19th century.

With our Love, we could save the world. –George Harrison (1943-2001)

Harrison was an English musician and singer-songwriter who achieved world fame as a guitarist with the musical group The Beatles.

Is it not by Love alone that we succeed in penetrating to the very essence of being? –Igor Stravinsky (1882-1971)

Stravinsky was a Russian, and later French and American composer, pianist and conductor.

Ultimately Love is everything. --M. Scott Peck (1936-2005)

Peck was an American psychiatrist and best-selling author best known for his book 'The Road Less Travelled'.

We're born alone, we live alone, we die alone. Only through our Love and friendship can we create the

illusion for the moment that we're not alone. –Orson
Welles (1915-1985)

Orson Welles was an American actor, director, writer and producer who worked extensively in theater, radio and film. He directed and starred in the film 'Citizen Kane' thought by many to be the greatest movie of all time.

The ultimate lesson all of us have to learn is unconditional Love, which includes not only others but ourselves as well. –Elisabeth Kubler-Ross (1926-2004)

Elisabeth Kubler-Ross was a Swiss-born American psychiatrist who pioneered the concept of providing psychological counseling to the terminally ill. Her book 'On Death and Dying' changed the way we treat the terminally ill.

I have found the paradox, that if you Love until it hurts, there can be no more hurt, only more Love… Let us always meet each other with a smile, for the smile is the beginning to Love. –Mother Teresa (1910-1997)

After receiving a message from God, Mother Teresa gave her life to the poor.

IV. Finale.

Someday, after mastering the winds, the waves, the tides and gravity, we shall harness for God the energies of Love, and then, for a second time in the history of the world, man will have discovered fire. –Pierre Teilhard de Chardin (1881-1955)

We have completed our journey and come to our destination point.

We have arrived at the place called Unconditional Love.

It has seemed that our journey has been a very long one.

But it has not been long when we compare the journey's length of time to eternity.

The spiritual evolution of humanity is complete.

The New Earth is manifested into reality.

So be it.

Thank you for reading these words.

###########

www.ingramcontent.com/pod-product-compliance
Lightning Source LLC
Chambersburg PA
CBHW070654290526
45790CB00001B/315